ESTATE PLANNING
&
LIVING TRUSTS
BLUEPRINT

The Complete and Easy-to-Follow Guide to Protecting Your Assets, Safeguarding the Future of Your Loved Ones, Optimizing Costs, & Creating a Lasting Legacy

by

Griffit Altman

Table of Contents

Welcome Onboard

Welcome to "Estate Planning and Living Trusts Blueprint"! We're thrilled that you've chosen to embark on this enlightening journey with us. This book is the culmination of an extensive endeavor—packed with diligent research, insights from interviews with seasoned experts, and a wholehearted devotion to sharing the most effective strategies in estate planning and living trusts. It has truly been a labor of love, fueled by our desire to empower you with knowledge that can significantly enhance your financial future. Before starting out here are 2 steps you can take:

Step 1) Access Your Bonus Content, go to the section at the end of the book titled 'Access Your Bonus Content' and follow the instructions

Step 2) Share how excited you are to begin this exciting adventure, we'd love to hear your initial thoughts. Here is what you can do:

Option A - Create a short video: Show off your new book and share your first impressions or expectations for what lies ahead.

Option B - Post a photo (or photos): Capture your copy of the book in a creative way and add a few words about your excitement.

Option C - Just Write: If you prefer to express yourself just in writing, a few thoughtful sentences reflecting your early views would be greatly appreciated.

Your feedback is invaluable; it helps others eager to grow and learn. Thank you for being a pivotal part of this journey. Please note that this is entirely optional.

Scan the QR code below to leave your review:

|Part 1| Getting the Basics

Section 1: Starting Out with Estate Planning

Defining Estate Planning

Welcome to the world of estate planning, a vital aspect of personal finance that frequently goes underappreciated until it becomes indispensable. Estate planning is a fundamental process that everyone should consider, regardless of the size of their assets. At its core, estate planning fundamentally entails preparing for overseeing and allocating your assets after your death or in the event of incapacitation, encompassing decisions on medical preferences when communication is not possible. It's about making sure your loved ones are looked after when you're not around and that your wishes are honored.

Estate planning can encompass many elements: wills, trusts, powers of attorney, healthcare directives, supplementary paperwork, and more. Every element fulfills a distinct role crucial to effectively managing all aspects of your affairs comprehensively. It's about laying down a clear roadmap for your family and legal representatives, guiding them on handling everything from your home to your financial obligations.

Why should everyone consider estate planning? Firstly, it provides peace of mind. Establishing a robust plan can ease the stress brought on by uncertainty about what lies ahead. Secondly, it helps avoid unnecessary legal hassles and financial burdens on your family, which can arise from probate or disputes among potential heirs.

Estate planning also offers you control over your financial legacy. Without a plan in place, state laws dictate the distribution of your assets, which might deviate from your desired intentions. By planning your estate, you decide who receives what, when, and how. Moreover, it allows you to provide for those who depend on you, including young children or relatives requiring special care.

A common misconception is that estate planning is only relevant for those approaching the end of their lives. However, life is unpredictable, and establishing an estate plan early can prepare you for unforeseen circumstances. Another misconception is the idea that estate planning is too complex and expensive for the average person. While it's true that estate planning can become complex, especially with larger or more diverse estates, the basics can be applied universally and affordably with professional guidance.

Remember, estate planning is a continuous process. As your situation evolves, your estate plan should adapt accordingly. Routine evaluations and adjustments in life milestones like getting married, having children, acquiring substantial assets, or changes in relationships are essential to maintaining an effective estate plan.

Getting started with estate planning doesn't have to be daunting. Begin considering your assets, which may include property, investments, insurance policies, and valuable personal items. Next, consider your family dynamics and the requirements of your potential heirs. Who depends on you financially? Do any of your family members require special considerations? Answers to these questions can guide you in structuring your estate plan!

Why is it Paramount for Everybody to Have an Estate Plan?

Estate planning is frequently associated with affluent individuals, dictating from plush offices about the distribution of their assets among their progeny. However, this is a narrow and somewhat misleading perspective. Estate planning is a crucial process for everyone, regardless of economic status, because it covers not only the disposition of assets after death but also important decisions during critical life events. Let's explore the fundamental reasons why having an estate plan is paramount for everyone.

1. Guaranteeing Your Assets Are Allocated According to Your Desires

The primary reason for having an estate plan is to guarantee that your assets, regardless of their size, are allocated according to your specific desires. If you don't have an estate plan, state intestacy laws will dictate the way your assets are distributed, and their choices may not match your preferences. For instance, in the absence of a will, a single person's assets might go to their parents or siblings when they would have preferred them to support a partner, a friend, or a charity.

2. Protecting Your Family and Loved Ones

Estate planning is fundamentally about protection—protecting your family and loved ones by providing for their future needs. If you have dependents such as a spouse, children, or other family members depending on your income, an estate plan allows you to secure their financial situation if something happens to you. This includes provisions for a surviving spouse, educational funds for children, and financial support for any dependents with special needs.

3. Minimizing Estate Taxes

Another compelling reason for estate planning is to reduce the amount taken from your estate by taxes. Proper estate planning can significantly decrease the taxes imposed on your estate, thus maximizing the amount your beneficiaries receive. Techniques like setting up trust accounts in the name of beneficiaries, making charitable donations from your estate, and structured gifting during your lifetime are just a few strategies that can lessen tax burdens.

4. Avoiding Probate

Probate can be an extended, public, and expensive legal procedure that your estate undergoes until is settled and distributed. By having a comprehensive estate plan in place, including the proper use of trusts, you can bypass probate and simplify the process of transferring assets. This means your heirs may gain access to your assets more quickly than if your estate went through probate.

5. Establishing Guardianship for Minor Children

No parent likes to think about not being there to raise their children, but establishing guardianship through an estate plan sets a clear directive on who should take care of your minor children if both parents pass away. Without such directives, the decision can end up in court, and a judge may choose someone you would not have selected.

6. Preparing for Illness and Incapacity

Estate planning also includes preparing for the possibility of your own incapacity before death. Documents like a durable power-of-attorney and healthcare directives (living wills) guarantee that your financial matters and healthcare choices are managed according to your preferences if you become incapacitated. This can be crucial in avoiding a situation where your loved ones are left to guess your intentions or, worse, are powerless to act on your behalf because the legal groundwork was not laid.

7. Supporting family members with special needs.

If you have part of your family or relatives with special needs, proper estate planning is essential. Without a specific plan, any direct inheritance could render them ineligible for benefits such as Social Security and Medicaid. Establishing a special needs trust guarantees their care without compromising their eligibility for government benefits.

8. Peace of Mind

A major advantage of having an estate plan is the profound feeling of assurance and tranquility it offers. Feeling that you have a plan in place that protects your family, directs your assets, and prepares for your own potential incapacity can relieve a great deal of stress and anxiety.

The significance of estate planning is immeasurable. It's essential for individuals to guarantee their intentions are honored and their close ones are looked after following their death. Estate planning establishes a definite path forward, relieves your family of undue stress during a difficult time, and safeguards your financial heritage.

Estate Planning Beginners FAQs

Embarking on estate planning can often seem daunting, especially if you're unfamiliar with the terminology and processes involved. To help demystify the subject and provide clarity, here's a comprehensive list of frequently asked questions (FAQs) that beginners often have about estate planning.

1. What exactly is estate planning?

Estate planning involves organizing the management and allocation of your assets both during and after your lifetime. Its main objective is to guarantee your assets are distributed as you desire, provide for your family and loved ones, and oversee your health and finances if you are unable to do so yourself.

2. Why is estate planning important?

Estate planning is vital because it empowers you to dictate asset distribution, protect your family's future, reduce tax liabilities, bypass probate, and designate a trusted individual to manage your affairs if you're incapacitated. Without an estate plan, these decisions can be made by courts without your input.

3. Which documents are usually part of an estate plan?

An estate plan generally includes several key documents:

- Will: Outlines your wishes regarding how your assets should be distributed and who will be guardians of minor children.

- Trusts: Assist in asset management during your lifetime and beyond, potentially circumventing probate.

- Durable Power of Attorney: Enables a chosen individual to handle your financial matters in case of incapacitation

- Healthcare Power of Attorney and Living Will: Directs your medical care if you cannot make decisions yourself.

- Beneficiary Designations: Secure the transfer of the specific assets or designated assets for specific heirs, like could be life insurance policies and retirement holdings.

- Guardian Designations: Identify who will take care of your minor children if you cannot.

4. Do you need a lawyer to create an estate plan?

While simple estate plans can sometimes be created with forms or online tools, it is usually wise to consult an expert estate planning attorney. This ensures that all documents are legally sound, reflect your wishes accurately, and consider all aspects of your personal and financial situation.

5. How does estate planning control my assets after I die?

Your estate plan outlines directives for managing your assets following your passing. This may involve designated gifts to individuals or organizations, as well as broader directives managed by a trustee or an executor, who ensures that your estate is distributed according to your will or trust documents.

6. What are the consequences if I haven't made an estate plan?

If you die without an estate plan, your assets are going to be allocated based on the intestacy laws governing your state. This often means your assets might be distributed in a manner that you wouldn't prefer. Furthermore, it can cause delays, additional expenses, and added stress for your surviving family members.

7. Is it possible to modify my estate plan once it has been established?

Absolutely. An estate plan must be regularly reassessed and revised in life milestones like getting married, going through a divorce, or having a child, substantial shifts in economic circumstances, or alterations in legal statutes. This ensures that your present desires are precisely mirrored and your family is sufficiently safeguarded.

8. How frequently should I reassess my estate plan?

In general, professionals advise revisiting your estate plan every three to five years, particularly after significant life events. This includes changes in marital status, the birth or adoption of a child, significant changes in financial situation, or when moving to a different state, as legal conditions affecting your estate plan may differ.

9. Are online estate planning services sufficient?

Online estate planning services can be a good start for some people, especially those with a straightforward situation. However, they might not offer customized advice or cater to complex scenarios like business ownership, special needs children, or significant tax considerations. Seeking guidance from a specialist ensures personalized advice and reassurance that every detail of your estate is expertly managed.

Gaining Momentum

After learning the essentials and understanding, you may be eager to get started but unsure of the practical steps to take. To begin effective estate planning, you must first thoroughly inventory all your assets. This goes beyond simply listing your significant possessions such as your house or vehicle. It requires a comprehensive look at everything you own that will need to be managed or passed on. Here's how to begin:

- Create a Detailed List: Start by listing all your physical and intangible assets. This includes real estate, vehicles, valuable personal property (jewelry, art, collectibles), bank accounts, stocks and bonds, retirement accounts, insurance policies, and any digital assets such as websites or digital currencies.

- Gather Important Documents: Collect all relevant financial documents such as bank statements, life insurance policies, real estate deeds, and recent tax returns. These documents will provide a clearer picture of your financial situation and are crucial for the next steps in estate planning.

- Consider Your Family Structure and Needs: As you inventory your assets, think about your family's needs and how you wish to address them in your estate plan. This may affect how you choose to distribute your assets.

Section 2: US Estate and Inheritance Taxes, Probate Process and Challenges

US Inheritance and Estate Taxes: Understanding the Basics

In estate planning, two critical types of taxes are relevant: inheritance tax and estate tax. Understanding these taxes, along with the exemptions available at the federal level, is crucial for anyone navigating estate planning:

Estate Tax: It is imposed on the overall worth of the defunct person's estate prior to being passed on to beneficiaries. The rate can vary by state and the relationship to the deceased, with closer relatives typically paying lower rates or nothing, while extended family members or unrelated individuals typically encounter elevated costs.

It is determined by the overall worth of the deceased individual's assets, encompassing cash, property, stocks, other assets. The federal government levies an estate tax determined by the estate's net worth, calculated after deducting debts and permissible deductions.

Inheritance Tax: In contrast to the estate tax, which targets the estate, the inheritance tax is imposed on those receiving the assets. While there isn't a federal inheritance tax, certain states impose this type of tax. The rate can depend on the state and the connection between the departed and the beneficiary. Closer relatives often pay less or none, compared to distant relatives or non-relatives.

To clarify in the United States, estate taxes are imposed federally and in some states, but not all states have this tax, making it crucial to comprehend the specific laws of the state in which one resides or owns property:

- Federal Tax: The federal government levies an estate tax determined by the entire value of the deceased's estate after certain deductions.

- State-Level Tax: Certain states levy their own estate or inheritance taxes, which can differ in rates and exemptions.

Types of Federal Exemptions: Lifetime and Annual

At the federal level, two primary types of exemptions help individuals manage potential estate tax liabilities:

- **Lifetime Exemption:** This allowance enables individuals to donate a certain amount during their life or as part of their estate upon death without sustaining federal estate taxes. In 2024, each individual can benefit from a federal estate tax exemption amounting to $13.61 million. If an individual's estate value is below this threshold, no federal estate tax is owed.

- **Annual Exemption:** Beyond the lifetime exemption, there is an annual allowance for gift tax. For 2024, an individual can give away until $18,000 per recipient yearly without these gifts accounting against their lifetime exemption or incurring any gift tax. This enables individuals to transfer portions of their estate during their lifetime without diminishing the threshold of their lifetime exemption.

The receiver of the gift does not need to be necessarily a child, grandchild or a relative to benefit from the exemption.

Navigating the Unlimited Marital Deduction in U.S. Federal Tax Laws

One of the most powerful tools you have at your disposal is the unlimited marital deduction provision of U.S. federal tax laws. This rule can profoundly impact your estate planning, enabling allows you to pass an unlimited amount of assets to your spouse tax-free. Similarly to navigating any tax law, it necessitates careful maneuvering to optimize its advantages.

The unlimited marital deduction is a feature in U.S. federal tax laws that permits the transfer of any amount of assets to your spouse at any time, including upon death, without triggering federal estate or gift taxes. This principle is vital in estate planning, enabling the postponement of estate taxes till the other spouse deceases too, thereby safeguarding the wealth intended for your heirs. To effectively use the unlimited marital deduction in your estate planning, you need to understand its mechanics. Here's how it works:

1. Transfers During Your Lifetime: You can give any amount of money or property to your spouse during your lifetime, without triggering federal gift taxes, as long as your spouse is a U.S. citizen.

2. Transfers at Death: Similarly, when you die, any assets included in your estate that you leave to your spouse are not subject to federal estate taxes at the time of your death assuming your spouse is a U.S. citizen. The assets can be transferred via your will, through a trust, or even under the laws of intestacy (if you die without a will).

3. Non-Citizen Spouse Considerations: In the event that your spouse is not a citizen of the United States, the unlimited marital deduction is not automatically available. You can still transfer assets, but you might need to establish a Qualified Domestic Trust (QDOT) to qualify for any marital deduction. You can find additional information in the trust section.

Here are several benefits that the unlimited marital deduction can provide in your estate planning:

- Tax Deferral: By transferring assets to your spouse, you defer any federal estate taxes on these assets until the passing of your partner. This may lead to substantial tax savings, particularly for large estates.

- Asset Protection: Transfers under the marital deduction can safeguard assets against potential creditors or legal issues, depending on how they are structured.

- Flexibility: This provision allows you to pass significant amounts of assets to your spouse in various ways, giving you flexibility in how you plan your estate.

To fully utilize the advantages offered by the unlimited marital deduction, explore these recommended approaches:

1. Direct Transfers: Simply leaving assets to your spouse in your will is the most straightforward approach to using the marital deduction.

2. Marital Trusts: You can create a marital deduction trust, often known as an "A" trust or "Marital Trust," to support your partner while retaining greater control on the final allocation of assets.

3. Life Insurance Policies: Life insurance payouts are typically considered part of your estate for tax calculations but leaving them to your spouse can often utilize the unlimited marital deduction to avoid this tax.

4. Gift Splitting: For married couples, gift splitting can allow you to double the annual gift tax exclusion amount by combining donations, and the limitless marital deduction ensures these transfers are not taxed.

While the unlimited marital deduction is beneficial, there are traps you need to avoid:

- Failure to Properly Title Assets: Ensure that assets are correctly titled, especially if you want them to pass directly to your spouse and qualify for the deduction.

- Overlooking State Estate Taxes: Some states have estate or inheritance taxes without a corresponding unlimited marital deduction. Be aware of your state's laws.

- Neglecting Proper Documentation: Always keep detailed records and proper documentation for all transfers, especially large ones, to ensure they qualify for the marital deduction.

- Not Planning for the Second Death: Remember, the marital deduction defers taxes, it doesn't eliminate them. Plan for what happens when your surviving spouse dies, as the assets will then be then added in their estate.

State-Level Estate and Inheritance Taxes

As of 2024, estate and inheritance taxes are administered at the state level in various forms across the United States, depending on specific state laws. Here's a summary of the relevant taxes in the states you're interested in:

- Connecticut, Hawaii, Illinois, Maine, Maryland, Massachusetts, Minnesota, New York, Oregon, Rhode Island, Vermont, Washington, and the District of Columbia enforce estate taxes within their jurisdictions.
- These states have different exemption thresholds, with some aligning to the federal exemption and others setting significantly lower limits.
- Maryland, New Jersey, and Pennsylvania impose both estate and inheritance taxes. Maryland is unique in that it has both taxes, with a flat inheritance tax rate of 10% on certain beneficiaries and an estate tax with its own exemption threshold.
- Iowa, Kentucky, and Nebraska solely impose inheritance taxes, which vary widely in terms of exemption amounts and tax rates. For example, Iowa has a progressive tax rate based on the relationship of the inheritor to the decedent, and Kentucky categorizes beneficiaries into different classes, each with varying rates and exemptions.

Understanding these taxes and exemptions is key for anybody in the scope of estate planning, empowering them to make knowledgeable decisions about handling and allocating their estate.

State	Estate Tax Exemption	Estate Tax Rate	Inheritance Tax	Inheritance Tax Rate
Connecticut	$9.1 million	Varied	No	N/A
Hawaii	$12.06 million	Varied	No	N/A
Illinois	$4 million	Varied	No	N/A
Maine	$5.8 million	Varied	No	N/A
Maryland	$5 million	Varied	Yes	10% (varies)
Massachusetts	$1 million	Varied	No	N/A
Minnesota	$3 million	Varied	No	N/A
New York	$6.11 million	Varied	No	N/A
Oregon	$1 million	Varied	No	N/A
Rhode Island	$1.648 million	Varied	No	N/A
Vermont	$5 million	Varied	No	N/A
Washington	$2.193 million	Varied	No	N/A
District of Columbia	$4 million	Varied	No	N/A
New Jersey	No estate tax	N/A	Yes	Varies by relation
Pennsylvania	No estate tax	N/A	Yes	0% to 15% (varies)
Iowa	No estate tax	N/A	Yes	0% to 15% (varies)
Kentucky	No estate tax	N/A	Yes	4% to 16% (varies)
Nebraska	No estate tax	N/A	Yes	1% to 18% (varies)

Section 3: How to Compute the Taxable Amount of an Estate

Understanding how to compute the taxable amount of an estate is key for estate planning and ensuring compliance with tax laws. The process involves several steps and considerations, including identifying the gross estate, deducting allowable expenses, and applying relevant deductions and exemptions.

1. Understanding the Gross Estate

The gross estate comprises all assets and interests possessed by the deceased at the moment of the passing, valued in its entirety.

This encompasses:

- Real estate properties

- Financial accounts, including checking, savings, and investment holdings

- Retirement holdings like IRAs and 401(k)s

- Life insurance policies (if the decedent owned the policy)

- Business interests, including shares in businesses and partnerships

- Personal property such as vehicles, jewelry, and artwork

2. Valuing the Gross Estate

To compute the gross estate, you must determine the fair market value (FMV) of these assets as of the time of death. The FMV is the market value at which the property would be sold under conditions where both parties are willing, not under pressure to buy or sell, and possess adequate knowledge of relevant information.

Example:

For a deceased homeowner, the FMV represents the current market selling price of the home.

3. Deductions from the Gross Estate

Funeral and Administrative Expenses

Costs resulting from the death of the deceased and the administration of the estate can be deducted. This includes:

- Memorial service and burial costs

- Administrative costs like legal and bookkeeping fees

- Executor's commissions

Debts and Mortgages

All debts that the passed person had at the time of their death can be deducted. This includes:

- Mortgages on property included in the estate

- Personal loans and credit card debts

- Medical bills related to the decedent's final illness

Losses During Estate Administration

Losses incurred during the administration of the estate, due to theft or casualty losses (like fire or flood damage), can also be deducted.

Marital Deduction

A key deduction is the marital deduction. This allows you to deduct the value of any property transferred from the deceased to their surviving spouse. This deduction is intended to protect the surviving spouse from substantial estate taxes at the first death.

- Requirement: The property must be transferred outright to the surviving spouse or to a qualifying trust (like a QTIP trust).

Charitable Deductions

Money or property donated to qualifying charities from the estate can be deducted. This deduction has no upper limit, so it can significantly reduce the estate's taxable amount.

State Death Taxes

Any estate or inheritance taxes paid to a state or the District of Columbia can be deducted.

---

4. Computing the Taxable Estate

Calculate the Adjusted Gross Estate

Subtract allowable deductions (funeral expenses, debts, losses, etc.) to determine the adjusted gross estate, you start with the gross estate and make the necessary adjustments.

Adjusted Gross Estate = Gross Estate - (Funeral Expenses + Debts + Losses)

Apply Marital and Charitable Deductions

Further reduce the adjusted gross estate by any amounts transferred to the surviving spouse or to charities.

Taxable Estate = Adjusted Gross Estate - (Marital Deduction + Charitable Deduction)

---

5. Lifetime Gift Adjustments

To determine the estate tax base, add up all the taxable gifts the deceased person made after 1976 that weren't included in the gross estate.

Estate Tax Base = Taxable Estate + Taxable Gifts

---

6. Applying Credits and Exemptions

Unified Credit

The unified credit covers both gift taxes and estate taxes. In recent years, the credit has effectively exempted a portion of the estate from being taxed. For instance, for estates of decedents dying in recent years, this exemption amount has been around $13.61 million per individual.

---

7. Compute Estate Tax

Apply the relevant tax rates to the estate tax base after subtracting the unified credit to find the preliminary federal estate tax.

State-Specific Considerations

Certain states enforce their own estate or inheritance taxes. In these cases, the state-specific exclusion amounts and tax rates also need to be considered. The federal estate tax credit for state death taxes can help lower the amount you owe in federal estate taxes.

Final Taxable Amount

The final step is to adjust for any remaining credits (like the credit for prior transfers or foreign death taxes) to compute the final estate tax due.

Final Estate Tax = Preliminary Estate Tax - Credits

Example Computation

Let's consider a hypothetical example to see how this works:

- Gross Estate Value: $15,000,000
- Funeral and Administrative Expenses: $200,000
- Debts and Mortgages: $300,000
- Property passed to the surviving spouse: $5,000,000
- Charitable Donations: $1,000,000
- Taxable Gifts (Post-1976): $500,000

1. Compute Adjusted Gross Estate:

   Adjusted Gross Estate = $15,000,000 - ($200,000 + $300,000) = $14,500,000

2. Apply Marital and Charitable Deductions:

   Taxable Estate = $14,500,000 - ($5,000,000 + $1,000,000) = $8,500,000

3. Adjust for Taxable Gifts:

   Estate Tax Base = $8,500,000 + $500,000 = $9,000,000

4. Apply Unified Credit (Assume 2024 Exemption $13.61M):

   Final Taxable Amount = $9,000,000 - $13,610,000 → less than zero   therefore no tax due if under exemption)

However, if the exemption were less, say $5 million:

Final Taxable Amount = $9,000,000 - $5,000,000 = $4,000,000

Then apply the estate tax rate (say 40% for the sake of example):

Estate Tax Due = 40% times $4,000,000 = $1,600,000

For more, information, check out the IRS website, or get in touch with an estate planning professional or consult the Internal Revenue Code.

Section 4: The Key Steps of the Probate Process

Probate is the formal procedure where the belongings of someone who has passed away are documented, debts are resolved, and possessions are distributed according to the individual's will or state laws (if there is no will). The process can be intricate and varies by state, but here are the key steps involved in most probate proceedings.

1. Filing of Petition and Notice to Heirs and Beneficiaries

The probate process begins with a petition to the probate court to authenticate the will and appoint an executor, or to appoint an estate administrator if no will exists. This request generally includes the death certificate and the original will (if accessible). Notice of the probate hearing must be given to all the deceased's heirs and beneficiaries as specified in the will, or, if no will exists, to statutory heirs according to state laws.

2. Appointment of Executor or Administrator

The court will appoint either the person named as executor in the will or an administrator if no will exists. This individual will bear legal responsibility for overseeing the management of the estate's matters. Their responsibilities involve gathering and organizing the deceased's belongings, resolving unpaid and taxes, and ultimately allocating possessions to those named as payees.

3. Inventory of the Estate

The executor or administrator must then create a list of the deceased person's belongings, which could encompass things like property, bank accounts, financial holdings, and other private possessions. This list of possessions is submitted to the court and usually involves assessments to determine how much certain belongings are worth.

4. Closing of Estate Debts and Taxes

Before passing on possessions to heirs, it's necessary to settle any remaining debts and taxes first. This includes funeral and burial costs, outstanding personal debts, and final income taxes. If the estate is large enough, federal and state estate taxes may also need to be paid (review the part on Estate and Inheritance Taxes for more details).

5. Legal Challenges or Will Contests

Heirs or other parties may challenge the will or certain provisions in the will. Challenges can be based on allegations that the will was made under duress, that the deceased was not mentally competent at the time the will was created, or that the will was forged or improperly executed.

6. Distribution of the Remaining Estate

After the totality of debts and taxes are settled, whatever is left of the person's belongings goes to their heirs as specified in their will. If there's no will, it follows the state's rules on who gets what. This often requires additional legal paperwork and sometimes court supervision.

7. Closing the Estate

The last step is to formally wrap up the estate in probate court. The executor or administrator will submit a conclusive report and request for distribution, outlining all financial activities carried out during the probate process. Once approved, assets are transferred to the beneficiaries, and the executor is discharged from their duties.

Detailed Considerations in the Probate Process

Legal and Financial Advice

Throughout the probate process, executors and administrators may need to consult with legal and financial experts. These experts offer advice on a range of matters, such as taxes, determining asset values, and understanding the legal consequences when distributing an estate.

Time and Costs

Probate can be time-consuming and costly, based on the estate's size and intricacy. Legal fees, court fees, executor fees, and costs associated with settling debts and taxes can diminish the estate's value.

Avoiding Probate

Many people choose to arrange their affairs to bypass probate. This can be achieved through mechanisms such as living trusts, joint ownership of assets, designation of beneficiaries on accounts like IRAs and insurance policies, and more. These strategies can help to move assets straight to heirs without the need for court intervention.

Hiring a Probate Lawyer

When you're faced with the task of managing a loved one's estate after their death, the probate process can seem daunting. This is where a probate lawyer comes in – someone who can guide you through the complex legal landscape, ensuring that your loved one's estate is resolved according to legal requirements and their preferences. Let's explore why you might need a probate lawyer, how to choose the right one, and how to work with them effectively.

As discussed, probate is the legal procedure for distributing a deceased person's estate to heirs and beneficiaries and settling any debts owed to creditors. It involves proving that the deceased's will is valid, determining and evaluating assets, settling debts and taxes, and ultimately allocating the leftover property based on the will or state law in the absence of one.

A probate lawyer, or an estate lawyer, helps you manage these steps. They provide legal advice, prepare and file the necessary documents with the probate court, manage the estate's assets, help pay debts and taxes, resolve income tax issues, and distribute the estate to the beneficiaries. If there are any disputes, the probate lawyer will represent the estate in court.

Why Hire a Probate Lawyer?

If your loved one's estate includes diverse assets, significant debts, or a complex family situation, you will benefit from the expertise of a probate lawyer. They can navigate the legal intricacies and ensure that every step of the process is handled correctly.

Probate lawyers are specialists in estate law, which is essential for addressing issues such as the validity of the will, the rights of various heirs, potential estate and inheritance tax liabilities, and handling creditors' claims against the estate.

By ensuring that the will is executed properly and in compliance with the law, a probate lawyer can help prevent potential disputes among beneficiaries, preserving family harmony during a challenging time.

The process of probate often takes a long time and can be quite complicated. A probate lawyer can streamline this process, enabling you to concentrate on personal issues amid challenging circumstances rather than getting bogged down in legal details.

Choosing a Probate Lawyer

Select a lawyer who specializes in probate, estate planning, and elder law. Their experience in handling estates similar to your loved one's will provide valuable insights and efficiencies.

Research the lawyer's reputation by reading their reviews and testimonials. A reputable lawyer will have a history of professionalism and success in handling probate cases. Websites like *avvo.com* or *martindale.com* can provide reviews and ratings for lawyers.

Select an attorney who promptly responds and communicates in a clear manner. Probate can be a lengthy process, and you need someone who will keep you informed and explain complex legal terms in a way that you can comprehend.

Learn how the lawyer charges for their services. Typical ways to bill for services include charging by the hour, setting a flat rate, or taking a percentage based on the estate's total value. Discuss these options and any extra costs, such as court fees or paperwork expenses. This conversation will help you budget for legal expenses and avoid surprises.

Working with a Probate Lawyer

Before your first meeting with a probate lawyer, gather all necessary documents, including the deceased's will, death certificate, list of assets and debts, deeds for real estate, and recent tax returns. This preparation will help the lawyer assess your situation more quickly and accurately.

During your first meeting, make sure to ask questions that help you grasp the process more thoroughly. Find out about the steps involved in the probate process, the expected duration, any references from past clients, and how the lawyer will communicate updates with you.

Ensure you fully comprehend the scope of the lawyer's services, how they will be paid, and the expected timeline. This agreement will avoid miscommunications and foster a seamless working relationship.

While the lawyer will handle most of the legal work, your involvement is crucial. Stay engaged in the process, and provide any requested information promptly to help move the process along efficiently.

For more detailed guidance, consider consulting resources like

https://www.americanbar.org/groups/real_property_trust_estate/resources/estate_planning/

|Part 2| Essential Documents

Section 5: Understanding Wills

When you're planning for the future, one of the most fundamental tools at your disposal is a will. This legal document is vital because it ensures that your belongings will be distributed as you want them to be after you're no longer here. Let's explore what a will is, why it's important, the different types you might consider, and how to choose an executor.

What Is a Will?

A will, often called a last will and testament, is a legal document that specifies how your belongings should be divided and how your children should be looked after once you're no longer here. By writing a will, you specify who should receive your property, whether it's your home, car, investments, or personal items, and you can also appoint a guardian for your children.

Your will serves as the guiding document for the executor, who is the person that guarantees the fulfillment of your wishes. If you don't have a will, the courts might end up making decisions about your estate, potentially distributing your assets according to state laws rather than what you would have wanted personally.

Reasons To Consider Having At Least a Will

Having a will is essential, regardless of your net worth, because it ensures that your wishes are heard and respected. Here's why it's important for you to have at least a basic will:

- Control Over Asset Distribution: You get to decide who gets what. Without a will, state regulations dictate the allocation of your assets, often resulting in a one-size-fits-all solution that might not suit your unique family dynamics or relationships.

- Guardianship of Minor Children: If you have children under 18, a will enables you to choose who will take care of them in case something happens to you. This can prevent potential custody battles and ensures your children are cared for by people you trust, in a manner you approve of.

- Minimize Legal Challenges: A well-written and legally sound will can help prevent disagreements among family members. It provides a clear statement of your intentions, helping to avoid misunderstandings and conflicts among those you leave behind.

- Speed Up the Probate Process: While having a will still involves probate (the court process of administering your estate), having a will can speed up this process and make it more straightforward, compared to dying intestate (without a will).

Different Types of Wills

Grasping the various types of wills aids in selecting the one that suits your needs best:

- Simple Will: This represents the simplest version of a will. In a simple will, you specify who will inherit your property and assets, and if applicable, you appoint a guardian for your minor children. This type of will is suitable if your estate is not large and your wishes are straightforward.

- Joint Will: Often used by married couples, a joint will is a single document that both parties sign, typically agreeing that when one spouse dies, the entirety of the estate passes to the surviving spouse, and then after the surviving spouse dies, the assets are distributed to the children. While joint wills can simplify the estate planning process, they can be restrictive, as the surviving spouse cannot later change the will.

- Living Will: Despite its name, a living will isn't actually a will for distributing assets. Instead, it's a written plan that details your wishes for medical care when you can't express them yourself, like during serious illness or if you're unable to communicate.

- Testamentary Trust Will: This type of will creates a trust when you die, and your assets are then transferred into this trust as per your instructions. It's useful if you want to provide for beneficiaries who are minors or who might need help managing their inheritance due to disabilities or other reasons.

- Pour Over Will: This will operates in tandem with a living trust. Essentially, it guarantees that any assets not transferred into your living trust during your lifetime will be transferred into the trust after your death through a process known as "pour-over." It's a safety net that catches any assets left out of the trust and guarantees they are allocated according to the conditions you established in the trust.

The Role of the Executor and How to Choose One

The executor of your will is tasked with executing your desires as detailed in your will. They are essential in handling the probate process, starting from submitting the will to the probate court to ensuring that your beneficiaries receive their rightful assets. Here are some considerations when selecting your executor:

- Responsibility and Trustworthiness: Select a person you have complete confidence in to act as your executor. They need to be responsible and organized, as they'll be managing your estate and navigating legal channels.

- Financial and Legal Acumen: Ideally, they should have some understanding of finance and law, or at least be capable of seeking and managing professional advice in these areas.

- Impartiality: It can be beneficial if your executor is somewhat neutral, especially if you anticipate any family conflicts. Sometimes, naming an executor outside the immediate family can reduce tension.

- Availability and Willingness: Make sure that who you choose wants and is capable to take on this role. Being an executor can demand considerable time and effort and sometimes challenging.

- Age and Health: Think about the age and healthiness of the candidate executor. Favor the ones who are younger than you and in excellent health to improve the chances that they will outlive you and be capable of performing their duties when required.

By carefully selecting your executor and clearly outlining your wishes in a will, you ensure that the process of distributing your estate goes as smoothly as possible, reflecting your desires and providing for those you care about in the best way possible.

Complications from Not Having a Will

Navigating life without a will can lead to numerous complications, particularly after you've passed away. Without this crucial document, you leave the distribution of your estate in the hands of state laws, and the consequences can be far-reaching, affecting not just your assets but also the emotional well-being of your loved ones. Understanding these potential complications can help you appreciate why having a will is essential for comprehensive estate planning.

When you pass away with no will, it is said to have died "intestate." When that happens (i.e. dying without a will), state intestacy laws will dictate the distribution of your assets. This process may pose challenges due to various reasons:

- Loss of Control Over Asset Distribution: Without a will, you have no say in who receives your assets. State laws typically distribute assets to your close family members, like your spouse and children, but this might not align with your personal wishes. For instance, you might have intended to leave something to a close friend or a charity, but without a will, these wishes won't be recognized.

- Potential Family Disputes: Not having a will can lead to disputes among your family members. When the state makes decisions on asset distribution, some relatives might feel they didn't receive their fair share or that the distribution doesn't reflect your actual wishes. These disputes can lead to lengthy, costly legal battles that can drain your estate's assets and create lasting rifts within your family.

- Guardianship Issues: With a will, you can designate a guardian for your minor children in the event of your death. Without a will, the courts decide who will raise your children, and the designated guardian may not align with your preferred choice.

Handling Complex Assets and Business Interests

For business owners or those with complex assets, dying without a will can be particularly problematic:

- Business Operations Can Be Jeopardized: If you run a business, not having a will can make it more difficult to plan for who will take over after you. Without clear directions, there could be a power vacuum in leadership, and the future of your business could be at risk. Your business might have to be sold or dissolved if there isn't a clear path to transfer ownership or manage operations after your death.

- Complicated Assets Are Harder to Manage: If you have assets in multiple states or countries, or if you own unique assets like digital properties or intellectual property, the absence of a will complicates managing these assets. Different jurisdictions have different laws, and without a will that specifically outlines your wishes, these assets could be subject to lengthy legal disputes.

To avoid these complications, here are some steps you can take:

1. Create a Will as Soon as Possible: The most straightforward way to avoid the complications of dying intestate is to create a will. Even a simple will can provide clear instructions about who should inherit your property and the management of your estate.

2. Regularly Update Your Will: Life changes, such as marriages, divorces, births, and acquisitions of new assets, mean your estate plan should evolve too. Keeping your will up-to-date ensures it always mirrors your latest wishes and life situation.

3. Work with an Estate Planning Attorney: Professional guidance is invaluable in estate planning. An attorney can assist in tackling complex matters and guarantee that your will is legally valid, and advise you on other estate planning tools like trusts that might be beneficial in your situation.

4. Communicate with Your Loved Ones: Ensure that your family members and other beneficiaries are informed about your estate plan and comprehend your intentions. Effective communication can help avoid confusion and disagreements among loved ones after you pass away.

5. Designate an Executor You Trust: Selecting a dependable and capable executor is essential. This person will oversee your estate's matters and guarantee that your preferences are executed precisely as outlined in your will. Your executor should be someone who is trustworthy, possesses strong organizational and communication abilities, and is prepared to handle the associated responsibilities.

Section 6: Health Care Directives

As you navigate through the process of estate planning, one of the most personal and vital components you need to consider is your health care directive. This goes beyond asset distribution; it's about ensuring your wishes known regarding your health care, especially in situations where you might not be able to speak for yourself. Two key documents should be considered, a Living Will and a Medical Power of Attorney.

Living Will

What Is a Living Will?

A living will is a legal document that specifies your preferences for medical treatment should you face incapacitation, guaranteeing that your decisions for end-of-life care are clearly communicated and honored. It's a way to guide your loved ones and doctors in making health care decisions based on what you would want, not what they think you might want.

Why It Is Useful and Why You Should Have One

Having a living will is invaluable because it provides clear instructions on how you want to be treated if you're seriously ill and there's no hope of recovery. For example, your living will can specify if you want life-sustaining measures such as ventilators or feeding tubes to be used or withheld if you're unable to survive without them. The clarity that a living will provides helps:

- Prevent Conflicts: It reduces the chances of disputes among your family members trying to guess your wishes. It can be agonizing for your loved ones to make these decisions without guidance, and your living will lifts this burden from their shoulders.

- Ensure Your Wishes Are Followed: It gives you a voice in your treatment, helping to ensure that medical professionals follow your preferences regarding end-of-life care, potentially preventing treatments that you would not want.

Complications in Case You Do Not Have One

Without a living will, the complications can be emotionally and financially draining:

- Family Disputes: Without your straightforward guidance, family members might disagree on the best way forward. These disputes can lead to severe conflicts and might even require court intervention to resolve.

- Unwanted Medical Treatment: You might receive medical care that goes against your wishes. In the absence of a living will, doctors will typically do everything possible to prolong your life, which might include invasive surgeries or treatments that you would not want.

How to Get One Done

1. Consult with Your Doctor: Understand the medical implications of your choices. It's essential to know what certain terms mean and how they apply to potential health situations.

2. Meet with an Attorney: While you can draft a living will yourself using forms, consulting with an attorney ensures that your living will meets legal standards and reflects your wishes accurately.

3. Be Specific: Clearly articulate your preferences about different types of medical care, including resuscitation, mechanical ventilation, tube feeding, and palliative care.

4. Sign and Notarize: Once drafted, make sure to sign your living will with witnesses and a notary present, as required by your state's laws.

5. Inform Your Family and Doctors: Make sure that your family members and primary care physician have copies of your living will and understand your wishes.

Medical Power of Attorney (Healthcare Proxy)

A medical power of attorney (also known as a healthcare proxy) is a legal document empowering a designated individual (your agent) to perform medical choices for you if you are incapacitated and incapable to make those decisions yourself. This person will work with healthcare providers to guarantee your medical care matches your wishes.

Why It Is Useful and Why You Should Have One

The utility of having a medical power of attorney includes:

- Continuous Representation: If you're incapacitated, you'll need someone who can quickly and effectively communicate your wishes to your healthcare providers. Your chosen representative has the authority to decide on treatments not specified in your living will.

- Flexibility: A medical power of attorney allows your agent to respond to unexpected situations and make decisions about new treatments or changes in your condition that your living will might not specifically address.

- Reduced Burden: It relieves your loved ones from the stressful responsibility of guessing your preferences on various medical treatments, as your agent will have clear authority to act on your behalf.

Complications in Case You Do Not Have One

Not having a medical power of attorney can lead to several issues:

- Lack of Authorized Decision-Maker: Without a designated agent, there might be no one with clear authority to make immediate decisions about your medical care, which can delay treatment in critical situations.

- Judicial Intervention: If there's no appointed agent, your relatives may need to seek court approval to act on your behalf, which may be lengthy and emotionally exhausting.

- Potential for Generalized Care: In the absence of a specific person to direct your care, medical professionals might opt for a more generalized approach to treatment that might not align with your specific wishes.

How to Get One Done

1. Choose Your Agent: Choose someone you have absolute trust in to decide on medical matters for you. This should be someone who shares your values and genuinely supports your interests.

2. Consult with an Attorney: While there are forms available, collaborating with an attorney can guarantee that your medical power of attorney is comprehensive and adheres to your state's legal requirements.

3. Discuss Your Wishes: Have an in-depth discussion with your selected representative regarding your medical preferences, values, and any directives you have about specific treatments or situations.

4. Complete and Sign the Document: Fill out the medical power of attorney form and sign it, typically in front of a witness or notary, depending on your state's laws.

5. Distribute Copies: Give a copy to your agent, your primary doctor, and perhaps a family member or close friend who might also be involved in your care.

Section 7: Understanding Financial Power of Attorney

One essential tool that you should be familiar with is the Financial Power of Attorney (POA). This legal document can significantly impact the management of your financial affairs should you become incapacitated unable to handle them yourself. Let's dive into what this means for you and why it's an important part of securing your future finances.

A Financial Power of Attorney is a legal instrument that permits someone you trust handle your financial affairs for you. This person, often denoted to as your agent or attorney-in-fact, is empowered to oversee your financial assets according to the permissions you outline in the document.

This role can include a wide range of responsibilities, from simple tasks like paying your bills to more complex duties like managing your investments, selling property, or conducting business transactions. Essentially, you're giving someone else the legal authority to handle your finances under the conditions you specify.

Why It Is Important and Why You Need One

Setting up a Financial Power of Attorney is key because life is unpredictable. Illness, injury, or unexpected events can strike without warning, leaving you unable to handle your finances. If you don't have a power of attorney (POA) set up:

1. Manage Your Finances: If you become incapacitated without a POA, no one can legally manage your finances without going to court. This could bring delays and additional costs as your close ones apply for the right to manage your affairs.

2. Continuity: With a POA, your financial matters can continue without interruption. Bills get paid, investment decisions are made, and your business operations can continue smoothly, which helps in maintaining your financial health and stability.

3. Control: A POA lets you choose who will manage your affairs. You can select someone who understands your financial goals and will act in your best interest, rather than leaving these decisions to a court-appointed guardian.

Types of Power of Attorney

Exploring different forms of Power of Attorney helps you select the one that suits your needs best:

1) Limited Power of Attorney: This form grants your agent the power to perform designated actions for you and for a limited period or under specific circumstances. For instance, you could assign a limited power of attorney to a friend to sell a car on your behalf while you are abroad.

2) Durable Power of Attorney: One of the most common and recommended types for estate planning. A durable power of attorney stays active as well in the event you become incapacitated, and it continues to be valid until you either revoke it or pass away. This continuity makes it especially useful for long-term planning.

3) Springing Power of Attorney: This POA activates solely if and when you become incapacitated, according to your specified criteria. While this offers more control and protection over when the POA activates, it can also lead to delays and complications since determining incapacity can require time and documentation.

Potential Complications in Case You Do Not Have One

Not having a Financial Power of Attorney can lead to several complications, especially if you become unable to manage your affairs:

- Legal and Financial Limbo: Your assets and financial affairs could be left in limbo. Bills may go unpaid, investments remain unmanaged, and important financial decisions are delayed, potentially leading to financial losses.

- Court-Appointed Guardianship: Your family may have to go through a legal process to appoint someone to take care of your affairs. This process can take a lot of time, money, and effort, and the court might not pick the person you want.

- Family Disputes: Without clear guidance from you, your family might clash over who should handle your financial affairs. Such disagreements can strain relationships and potentially escalate into legal conflicts., compounding the stress and challenges during an already difficult time.

How to Get One Done

To establish a Financial Power of Attorney that reflects your wishes and protects your interests, you should:

1. Choose Your Agent Carefully: Select someone you trust deeply to manage your financial affairs. This should be someone you can count on, who understands finances well, and will always prioritize your best interests.

2. Consult with an Attorney: While templates and forms are available, consulting with an attorney ensures that your POA meets all legal requirements and is tailored to your specific needs. A lawyer can clarify the consequences of each type of POA and guide you in making the best choice.

3. Be Specific: Clearly outline what powers your agent will have. Specify if you're setting up a durable, limited, or springing POA. When you give clear and detailed instructions, your agent can do a better job of assisting you.

4. Sign and Notarize: Most states require that your POA be signed in the presence of a notary and witnesses. This step formalizes the document, making it legally binding.

5. Communicate: Make sure your agent and key family members know where to find your POA and understand your plans. Being transparent helps avoid misunderstandings and makes sure everyone is ready if the document needs to be used.

By setting up a Financial Power of Attorney, you are taking a proactive step to ensure that your financial matters are handled smoothly and in line with your wishes, as well if you're not capable to oversee them yourself. This planning is more than just protecting your assets—it's about giving you and your people peace of mind. It's about making sure your financial legacy is handled wisely, no matter what the future brings.

Section 8: Guardianship Designation

Guardianship designation constitutes a key element of estate planning, especially for parents and caregivers. It ensures your dependents, especially minor children, are looked after by someone you trust if you become unable to do so. This part of your estate plan requires thoughtful consideration and clear legal documentation to offer reassurance for you and your family.

A guardianship designation is a formally recognized document that appoints a person to take over the care of your minor children or dependents if you die or become incapacitated. This person, known as the guardian, is given the power to make decisions for the child's welfare, education, and overall upbringing.

This designation can cover both the guardianship of the person, meaning the daily care and decisions for the child, and the guardianship of the estate, meaning the management of the child's finances and property. It brings peace of mind knowing that your children are looked after by someone you trust, ensuring consistency and stability in their lives during a challenging time.

Why It Is Important, in What Cases, and Why You Need One

Having a guardianship designation is crucial for several reasons. First and foremost, it provides a clear plan for your children's care, preventing confusion and possible disputes among family members. If no guardian is designated, the court will determine who will care for your children, potentially against your wishes.

In cases where you are a single parent, have a blended family, or if both parents might be incapacitated or deceased at the same time, a guardianship designation becomes even more vital. It ensures that your children are placed with someone who knows them, understands their needs, and is committed to providing a loving and stable environment.

By specifying a guardian, you also help reduce the emotional stress and legal complexities that can arise during such transitions. This foresight can make a significant difference in how your children cope with the loss and adjust to their new living arrangements.

Types of Guardianships

Different types of guardianship are available, each tailored to meet specific needs and situations:

- Permanent Guardianship: This type of guardianship is designed to be long-term and typically remains in place until the child reaches adulthood. It is suitable when the parents are no longer able to care for the child due to death or severe incapacitation.

- Temporary Guardianship: Sometimes called interim or emergency guardianship, this type is set for a limited period and is useful in situations where the parents might be temporarily unable to care for their children due to illness or other short-term issues. It provides immediate care while longer-term arrangements are being made.

- Standby Guardianship: This type of guardianship allows a parent to designate someone to step in as guardian upon the parent's incapacity or death without immediate court intervention. It provides a smooth transition and ensures that the designated guardian can assume their role without delay.

Understanding the differences and implications of each type of guardianship helps you make well-informed choices to best address the needs of your children and family dynamics.

The Legal Framework for Guardianship

The legal framework for guardianship varies by jurisdiction but generally involves several key steps to ensure that the process is clear and legally binding. You will need to draft a guardianship designation document that outlines your choice of guardian and the specific responsibilities they will have. This document must comply with state laws and typically requires the signatures of the parent or parents, the proposed guardian, and witnesses.

The court system oversees the process to ensure that the appointed guardian is suitable and that the best interests of the child are considered. This might involve a court hearing where the judge reviews the designation and any objections from other family members or interested parties.

Formalizing guardianship is not just about naming someone in your will; it's about ensuring that the designation is recognized and enforceable by law. This encompasses also registering the guardianship designation with the suitable legal establishments, especially if you are creating a standby guardianship that requires immediate activation upon certain conditions.

How to Choose the Right Guardian

Selecting the best guardian for your children is among the most crucial choices you'll make when planning your estate. This person will take charge of the care, upbringing, and well-being of your children if you are no longer able. Choosing the right person is essential. They should share your values and parenting approach, and be ready and capable of taking on this important role.

When choosing a guardian, consider factors beyond just familial relationships. Here are some key aspects to think about:

Values and Beliefs: Select someone whose values, beliefs, and parenting style are similar to your own. This alignment ensures that your children are raised in an environment that reflects the principles and morals you consider important.

Emotional and Physical Ability: The prospective guardian must possess the emotional and physical ability required to assume the responsibility. Consider their health, age, and energy levels to ensure they can provide the care and support your children need.

Financial Stability: While the guardian doesn't have to be wealthy, they should be financially stable and have the ability of managing the additional financial mission associated with raising children.

Relationship with Your Children: It's beneficial if the guardian already has a strong, positive relationship with your children. This familiarity can ease the transition and provide emotional stability for your children during a difficult time.

Location and Lifestyle: Consider the guardian's location and lifestyle. If they live far away, this could mean a significant change for your children, including new schools, friends, and community. Ensure that their lifestyle is conducive to raising children and aligns with what you envision for your child's upbringing.

Willingness to Serve as Guardian: It's crucial to have a candid conversation with the potential guardian about the responsibilities and expectations. They need to be genuinely willing to take on the role, understanding the long-term commitment it involves.

How to Formalize a Guardianship Designation

Once you have chosen a guardian, the next step is to formalize your decision legally. Here's how to go about it:

Drafting the Document: Collaborate with an estate planning counsellor to draft a guardianship designation in compliance with state laws. This document should clearly state your choice of guardian and any specific instructions regarding the care of your children.

Including in Your Will: Ensure that your guardianship designation is included in your will. This provides a clear, legally binding record of your wishes.

Signing and Witnessing: The guardianship designation must be signed by you and witnessed or notarized as required by state law. This step is crucial to make sure the document can be upheld in a court of law.

Informing Key Parties: Inform your chosen guardian, family members, and close friends about your decision. Provide them with copies of the designation so they are aware of your wishes.

Registering with the Court: In some states, you may need to file the guardianship designation with the local probate court. Your lawyer can help you navigate this process to make sure everything gets documented correctly.

Regular Reviews: Since life situations evolve, regularly reassessing and modifying your guardianship designation accordingly. Ensure that your choice of guardian still reflects your wishes and that the designated person remains willing and able to serve.

How to Discuss Guardianship with Potential Candidates

Discussing guardianship with potential candidates is a sensitive but necessary conversation. Here's how you can approach it:

Be Honest and Clear: Explain why you are asking them to take on this responsibility and what it entails. Make sure you clearly communicate what you expect and provide specific instructions for how you want your children to be cared for.

Discuss Practicalities: Talk about the practical aspects, such as living arrangements, financial support, and any potential challenges. Ensure they grasp the complete extent of what's required.

Listen to Their Concerns: Give them the opportunity to voice any worries or hesitations they may have. This open dialogue helps ensure they are fully committed and prepared to take on the role if needed.

Provide Reassurance: Reassure them that they will have support from other family members and friends and that you will make provisions in your estate to help with the financial burden.

Document the Agreement: Once they agree, document their consent formally. This might involve having them sign a statement of acceptance that is included with your legal documents.

Difference Between Child Medical Consent and Guardianship

Grasping the distinction between child medical consent and guardianship is paramount:

- Child Medical Consent: This gives someone temporary permission to make medical decisions for your child when you're not around. It's typically used for short-term situations, like when you are traveling.

- Guardianship: This is a more permanent arrangement that gives someone the legal authority to care for your child and make all decisions related to their welfare, including medical, educational, and financial decisions. Guardianship is intended for long-term care and involves a more comprehensive transfer of parental rights and responsibilities.

Section 9: Letter of Intent, Just In Case Instructions & End Of Life Directives

Estate planning involves more than simply creating legal paperwork such as wills and trusts—it's about preparing for the future, ensuring your wishes are clearly communicated and ensuring the people you care for are safeguarded according to your wishes. Among the various tools at your disposal, a Letter of Intent, Just In Case Instructions, and End of Life Directives provide personal, practical, and heartfelt guidance. Let's start by exploring the Letter of Intent.

Letter of Intent

A Letter of Intent (LOI) is a personal document that accompanies your formal estate planning paperwork. While it is not legally binding, it serves as a guide to your executors, trustees, and loved ones, offering insight into your wishes, values, and the rationale behind your decisions. The LOI bridges the gap between legal formalities and personal touch, ensuring your estate plan is implemented in a way that corresponds with your intents and the unique dynamics of your family.

Conveying Love and Gratitude

The LOI is an opportunity to express your love and gratitude to your family and friends. Begin by directly speaking to your loved ones, expressing genuine gratitude for their existence in your life. Acknowledging the special relationships and memories you've shared can provide comfort and a sense of connection. This personal touch reminds your loved ones of your enduring love and gratitude, even in your absence.

Personal Stories and Memories

Include your own personal anecdotes and memories that emphasize important moments and relationships. These anecdotes not only honor your loved ones but also offer a glimpse into your life and values. Sharing these memories can bring joy and solace to those left behind, helping them feel closer to you and preserving your legacy in a meaningful way. Reflect on experiences that shaped your life, lessons learned, and the impact your loved ones had on you.

Explanation of the Decisions

Your LOI should also explain the reasoning behind your estate planning decisions. This is particularly important for choices that might not be immediately understood by your heirs. For example, if you decided to allocate a greater share of your possessions to one of your child over another due to specific needs or circumstances, provide a clear and compassionate explanation. This openness helps ensure that your beneficiaries understand clearly, reducing the chances of confusion or disagreements.

Sharing Your Values and Principles

Your values and principles are integral to who you are, and sharing them in your LOI ensures they continue to guide your family. Discuss the beliefs and values that have shaped your life and decisions. Whether it's the importance of education, charitable giving, hard work, or family traditions, articulating these principles helps your loved ones understand the foundation of your choices and the legacy you wish to leave behind.

Message for the Future

End your LOI with a message for the future. Offer words of wisdom, encouragement, and love to your family as they move forward without you. This message can be an enduring source of motivation and guidance, helping your loved ones navigate their own lives with the values and principles you cherished. Encourage them to support each other, pursue their dreams, and live lives that honor your memory.

Just In Case Instructions

Just In Case Instructions are a comprehensive set of directives that cover various aspects of your life and estate. JICs are designed to be practical and immediately actionable. They provide your loved ones with the information and instructions they need to manage your personal and financial affairs effectively during an emergency. By preparing these instructions, you ensure that your loved ones can handle unexpected situations with confidence and clarity.

List of Critical Contacts

One of the first components of your JIC should be a list of critical contacts. This list includes the names, phone numbers, email addresses, and relationships of key individuals who should be notified in an emergency. These contacts might include family members, close friends, neighbors, your employer, and essential professionals such as your lawyer, financial advisor, and healthcare providers. Providing this information ensures that your loved ones know who to reach out to for support and assistance.

Addresses

In your JIC, include the addresses of all relevant properties, such as your home, vacation homes, rental properties, and any other locations where you have significant interests. Clearly specify which address corresponds to which property, and include any pertinent details that might be helpful, such as the location of keys, security codes, and instructions for accessing the property. This information is crucial for managing your real estate and ensuring that all your properties are secure and well-maintained during an emergency.

How to Access Accounts

Accessing your financial accounts is a critical part of managing your affairs. Your JIC should provide detailed instructions on how to access all your financial accounts, including bank accounts, investment accounts, retirement funds, and any online payment systems or digital wallets you use. Include usernames, passwords, security questions, and any other necessary credentials. You might want to use a secure password manager to keep this information safe. Make sure to share the master password with your designated executor. This ensures that your loved ones can manage your finances without facing unnecessary obstacles.

Where to Find Key Documents

Knowing the location of key documents is essential for handling your affairs efficiently. Your JIC should specify where to find important documents such as your will, trust documents, insurance policies, property deeds, car titles, and tax returns. Additionally, include information on where to find your birth certificate, marriage certificate, Social Security card, and any other critical personal documents. By clearly indicating the location of these documents, you help your loved ones avoid confusion and delays in managing your estate.

High-Level Financial Overview

Providing a high-level financial overview gives your loved ones a clear picture of your financial situation. This overview ought to contain a summary of your assets and liabilities, such as bank information, financial holdings, real estate, outstanding loans, and credit card unpaid. Include the names of financial institutions, account numbers, and any relevant contact information. This summary assists your family and friends in grasping your financial situation, enabling them to make well-informed choices regarding your estate management.

What to Do for Dependents with Special Needs

If you are responsible for dependents who require special care, your JIC should include specific instructions for their care. This might involve detailed information about their daily routines, medical needs, dietary requirements, and preferred activities. Make sure to give the contact details for their healthcare providers, therapists, and any other caregivers who are involved in their treatment. Additionally, include details about any financial arrangements or trusts set up to support them. These instructions ensure that your dependents continue to receive the care and support they need in your absence.

What to Do with Pets

Pets are an important part of your family, and your JIC should include instructions for their care. Specify who should take care of your pets, along with detailed information about their feeding schedules, medical needs, and any behavioral quirks. Provide contact information for your veterinarian and any pet sitters or boarding facilities you use. This ensures that your pets are well-cared for and experience as little disruption as possible during an emergency.

Other Access Instructions

Finally, include instructions for accessing other important assets and locations, such as safes, safe deposit boxes, and storage units. Provide the necessary keys, combinations, and access codes, and specify where these items can be found. This guarantees that your loved ones can obtain and manage all your valuable possessions without unnecessary difficulty.

Memorial Preferences and End of Life Directives

A Memorial Preference document sometimes also called End of Life Directive helps detail how you would like to be celebrated after your death. This can include the type of funeral or memorial service you desire, specific rituals or traditions, and any special requests you may have.

How Would You Like to Be Celebrated

When thinking about how you would like to be celebrated, consider the values and traditions that are important to you. This might include cultural, religious, or personal preferences that reflect your identity and how you wish to be remembered. Your memorial preferences provide an opportunity to create a meaningful and comforting experience for your loved ones, helping them to honor your memory in a way that feels authentic to you.

Begin by thinking about what truly matters to you and the legacy you wish to create. Do you want your celebration to be a joyous occasion that celebrates your life, or a more somber and reflective event? Consider including specific rituals or activities that are meaningful to you. This might be a particular type of music, readings from favorite books or poems, or cultural traditions that you want incorporated into the service.

Type of Funeral or Memorial Service

Deciding on the type of funeral or memorial service is a significant part of your End of Life Plan. This decision can be influenced by personal, religious, or cultural beliefs. Here are some options to consider:

- Traditional Funeral: Typically, this involves a gathering or wake where people come together, followed by a formal service held at a funeral home or place of worship, and concluding with the burial. Specify whether you prefer an open or closed casket, and any particular religious or cultural rites you want included.

- Memorial Service: A memorial service usually occurs following the burial or cremation and can be hosted in various locations. It is a flexible option that allows for a more personalized celebration of your life, without the constraints of a traditional funeral.

- Cremation: If you prefer cremation, specify what you want done with the ashes. You can choose to keep them in an urn, scatter them in a place that holds special meaning, or even incorporate them into a piece of jewelry or artwork as a memorial.

- Green Burial: For those concerned about environmental impact, a green burial is an eco-friendly option that avoids embalming chemicals and often uses biodegradable caskets.

- Celebration of Life: This service aims to honor and cherish your life instead of emphasizing sadness over your passing. It can be held in any location and might include music, dancing, and sharing stories about your life.

Additional Considerations

Beyond the type of service, there are several additional considerations to include in your End of Life Directive and Memorial Preferences:

- Obituary: Provide guidance on how you would like your obituary to be written, including key achievements, personal values, and messages to your loved ones. Specify where you want it published.

- Personal Messages: Consider leaving personal messages for family and friends. These can be included in your directive or in separate letters to be delivered after your passing.

- Charitable Donations: If you would like to honor the memory with donations to a particular charity instead of sending flowers, feel free to include this preference. Provide details about the charity and why it's important to you.

- Eulogy and Readings: Indicate who you would like to deliver your eulogy and any specific readings or music you want included in the service. This helps personalize the event and ensures it reflects your life and values.

- Special Requests: Any other special requests or instructions should be detailed here. This might include specific attire for your service, a particular location for your burial or scattering of ashes, or unique rituals that are meaningful to you.

|Part 3| Understanding Trusts

Section 10: Introduction to Trusts

A trust is essentially a legal set-up where a trustee oversees assets for another person or group, known as the beneficiary, for their benefit. This setup is typically created by a third party, often referred to as the grantor, settlor, or trustor. Trusts are carefully designed to make certain that assets are overseen, protected, and allocated in alignement with the trustor's intentions, providing dependable oversight and support.

Now, let's break down the types of trusts you might encounter, focusing primarily on the distinction between living and non-living trusts:

- Living Trust (Inter Vivos Trust): A living trust is created while the person who establishes it is still alive. It is shaped as either revocable or irrevocable, that means it can be amended or dissolved as long as the trustor is alive, or it can be set in a way that it cannot be changed.

- Non-Living Trust (e.g. Testamentary Trust): This type of trust is established through a will after the death of the trustor. It comes into effect only upon the trustor's passing and is irrevocable, as it cannot be altered once the trustor is deceased.

The Roles Involved in a Trust

Understanding the roles within a trust setup is crucial to recognizing how trusts function:

- Grantor/Settlor/Trustor: This is the individual who establishes the trust, deciding how the assets within the trust should be managed and specifying the beneficiaries.

- Trustee: the one or entity chosen to oversee and handle the assets held in trust. This role requires managing the assets prudently and in accordance with the trust documents and the trustor's wishes.

- Beneficiary: Beneficiaries are those who receive the benefits from the trust, which can include income or other rights to the trust assets specified by the trustor.

Main Categories of Trusts

Trusts exist in different types, each designed to serve specific strategic goals in estate planning:

- Revocable Trusts: Trusts are frequently valued for their adaptability, allowing the person who establishes the trust to make changes or cancel it while they're alive.

- Irrevocable Trusts: These are used for their tax benefits and asset protection features, as they generally cannot be altered once established.

- Asset-Protection Trusts: These trusts are created to safeguard assets from creditors and are usually irrevocable, offering a robust safeguard for the assets held within them.

- Special Needs Trusts: These trusts make sure that people who receive government benefits can inherit money without losing their eligibility.

Section 11: Benefits of Using Trusts

Avoiding Probate

A major benefit of incorporating trusts in estate planning is their capacity to bypass the probate process. Probate is typically public, can take a considerable amount of time and expensive legal procedure that entails the verification of a defunct person's will, closing debts, and allocating the residual assets to the rightful heirs. Trusts, particularly living trusts, allow assets to pass outside of probate, offering a smoother and more private transition of assets to beneficiaries. How Trusts Bypass Probate:

- When you establish a trust, you transfer ownership of your assets from your personal estate to the trust. Upon your death, these assets are already positioned within a legal structure that does not require probate to dictate their distribution.

- The trustee you've appointed, often the same person as the settlor or grantor, can directly manage and distribute the assets as stipulated in the terms set out in the trust without requiring judicial involvement, which can reduce the time needed, reduce expenses and keep personal matters out of the public record.

Tax Benefits

Trusts can also offer substantial tax advantages, which can be utilized to optimize the overall tax obligation of the estate and the beneficiaries. Estate Tax Reductions:

- Irrevocable Trusts: Assets placed in an irrevocable trust are typically excluded from the grantor's taxable estate. This exempts them from estate taxes upon the grantor's death, potentially yielding substantial tax savings, particularly for wealthy individuals.

- Charitable Trusts: These bring estate tax benefits through charitable deductions. For example, assets placed in a charitable remainder trust can lower your taxable estate by the value of the charitable donation, while also providing an income stream during your lifetime.

Gift Tax Implications

- Trusts allow for strategic gifting that uses the annual gift tax exclusion and the lifetime gift tax exemption more effectively. For instance, a grantor can place assets into a trust and make annual tax-free gifts to the beneficiaries through the trust, utilizing the annual exclusion limit ($18,000 per recipient in 2024).

Asset Protection

Trusts serve as a robust instrument for safeguarding assets from creditors, lawsuits, and judgments, making sure that beneficiaries receive their intended inheritance without external interferences. Protection Mechanisms:

- Spendthrift Provisions: Many trusts include spendthrift clauses that prevent creditors of a beneficiary from claiming the beneficiary's future inheritance to satisfy debts. This protection ensures that trust assets are only distributed according to the terms of the trust and cannot be accessed by creditors.

- Discretionary Trusts: These trusts grant the trustee the authority to allocate funds to beneficiaries at their discretion. Since distributions are not automatic or mandatory, these assets are generally beyond the reach of creditors until they are actually distributed.

- Charitable Trusts: Established to offer funding to a charitable organization, while also enable to optimize trustor's tax. These can be set up as remainder trusts, where the trust assets revert to the charity after a specified period, or lead trusts, where the charity receives benefits for a period before the remainder goes back to the trustor's heirs.

Section 12: Steps to Establish a Trust

Step 1: Define Your Goals

Before establishing a trust, it's crucial to clearly articulate your objectives and what you aim to accomplish. Whether it's asset protection, tax planning, providing for a loved one, or supporting charitable causes, your goals will identify the trust type that aligns best with your needs.

- Considerations: Think about whom you want to benefit, how you want the assets managed, and the control level you wish to retain.

Step 2: Choose the Type of Trust

Aligned with your objectives, choose the appropriate type of trust. Each category serves unique purposes, providing different levels of control and flexibility to cater to diverse needs.

- Revocable Trust: Lets you retain control of your assets during your lifetime and adjust the trust terms if needed.

- Irrevocable Trust: Once set up, this type of trust cannot be changed. It's commonly employed to reduce estate taxes and safeguard assets.

- Special Needs Trust: Created to support individuals with disabilities by meeting their needs without affecting their eligibility for government aid.

- Charitable Trust: Enables you to contribute to charitable causes and at the same time gaining tax advantages and potentially supporting non-charitable beneficiaries.

Step 3: Select the Trustee

Deciding who will be your trustee is crucial when setting up a trust, as it's one of the most significant choices you'll make. The trustee will oversee the trust's assets and make sure that the trust's instructions are followed as intended.

- Responsibilities: Tasks include overseeing and investing the trust's assets, disbursing funds to beneficiaries, and maintaining precise financial records.

- Selection Criteria: The trustee should be someone you trust implicitly, who is also financially savvy and has a good understanding of fiduciary duties. You might also prefer a professional trustee, like a bank or trust firm, to oversee your affairs.

Step 4: Identify the Beneficiaries

Clearly identify who will benefit from the trust. Beneficiaries include family members, friends, charitable organizations, or anyone else who may benefit.

- Specificity: Define how and when beneficiaries will get the trust resources. Consider any rules or stipulations you want to place on their receipt of the benefits.

Step 5: Create the Trust Document

Collaborate with a seasoned estate planning lawyer to create the trust paperwork. This legal document will detail every aspect of the trust, including its terms, the powers granted to the trustee, the rights of beneficiaries, and the specific conditions that govern how the trust functions.

- Key Elements: Must include the trust's name, purpose, detailed instructions for distributions, and the powers granted to the trustee.

Step 6: Fund the Trust

To ensure a trust operates effectively, it needs to have sufficient funding. You will need to transfer assets into the trust, which may include bank accounts, real estate, stocks, or other assets.

- Transfer Documents: Depending on the asset type, this might involve changing titles or deeds, designating the trust as a beneficiary, or endorsing certificates.

Step 7: Execute the Trust

With all elements in place, execute the trust document. This typically requires notarization and possibly witnesses, depending on state laws.

- Legal Formalities: Guarantee compliance with all legal stipulations to make the trust legally binding.

Step 8: Manage the Trust

After the trust is initiated, ongoing management is key to its success. This comprises administering the trust according to its terms, investing assets prudently, making distributions as specified, and preparing annual tax returns.

- Ongoing Review: Regular reviews of the trust's terms and its financial performance are crucial, especially to adapt to any changes in the law or in the beneficiaries' circumstances.

Section 13: The Importance of Pour Over Wills

A pour-over will is an essential document in comprehensive estate planning, particularly for those who have established a trust. It's a unique form of will that works alongside a living trust, designed for specific legal and financial purposes. Its primary function is to catch any assets that have not been explicitly placed into the trust while the trustor is alive. At the time of the trustor's death, the pour-over will effectively "pours" these assets into the trust, from which they are distributed according to the trust's terms. Unlike a traditional will, which directly specifies how all assets should be distributed, a pour-over will simply transfers all remaining personal assets into an already established trust upon death.

Importance of a Pour-Over Will

1. Ensures All Assets Are Included in the Trust: Even with meticulous planning, it's common for some assets to be inadvertently left outside of a trust. A pour-over will makes sure that any assets you might have missed are included in your estate plan and distributed according to how you've specified in your trust.

2. Simplifies Estate Planning: By ensuring that all assets funnel into the trust, a pour-over will simplifies the management of your estate upon your death. This could especially benefit by making things simpler for the person carrying out the will and those who inherit.

3. Enhances Privacy: Since the assets will be moved to a trust, which is exempt from the public scrutiny of probate (in most cases), a pour-over will can help maintain privacy concerning the details of your estate.

What Should a Pour-Over Will Contain?

1. Declaration and Revocation: Like any will, it should open with a declaration that the document is your will, including a revocation of all previous wills and codicils.

2. Identification of the Trust: The will must clearly state which trust will receive the assets. This information typically covers the trust's name, when it was set up, and may also mention who the trustees are.

3. Comprehensive Asset Inclusion: While specific bequests might still be mentioned, the crucial language in a pour-over will states that all remaining assets not otherwise accounted for should transfer to the trust.

4. Executor Appointments: It should appoint an executor that will oversee the estate's matters after your death, ensuring that assets are properly funneled into the trust.

5. Guardianship Provisions: If applicable, particularly for those with minor children, the will should specify guardianship provisions to ensure that children are cared for by trusted individuals.

6. Signatures and Attestations: The will must be signed in the presence of witnesses, fulfilling the state's legal requirements to be considered valid.

Strategic Considerations

1. Coordination with Trust Documents: The pour-over will should be fully coordinated with the related trust documents to ensure consistency and clarity in estate execution.

2. Regular Updates: It's key to regularly review and possibly amend your pour-over will as life circumstances change, such as the when you have a child, getting married, divorcing, or significant move in the stat of the assets.

3. Legal Compliance: It is key to ensure that the pour-over will observe the state laws to avoid any potential challenges during probate.

Section 14: Revocable vs. Irrevocable Trusts - Understanding Flexibility and Control

When you're preparing your estate, choosing between a revocable and an irrevocable trust is a crucial choice you'll need to make. This decision will affect how much control you retain over your assets, their protection, the flexibility of the plan, and the tax impact.

What Are Revocable and Irrevocable Trusts (reminder)

A revocable trust, or living trust, is a flexible set-up that can be modified or terminated throughout your lifetime. The person establishing the trust is referred as the grantor, in this position you keep authority of the assets held in the trust and can amend its terms or terminate it completely.

Unlike revocable trusts, you can't change or end an irrevocable trust without the agreement of the trust's beneficiaries after it's set up. The implication is that once you place assets in an irrevocable trust, basically you effectively relinquish your ownership and control over those assets.

Comparison of Flexibility and Control

Flexibility

- Revocable Trusts: can be amended easily, allowing you to modify the trust's terms in response to new situations in your life.

- Irrevocable Trusts: Lack of flexibility since changes cannot be made once the trust is established, which can be a drawback if your situation or intentions change.

Control Over Assets

- Revocable Trusts: You retain complete management of your assets throughout your life (in case you name yourself as Trustee). You can decide how the assets are invested, distributed, or reclaimed.

- Irrevocable Trusts: When you create a trust, you transfer control of your assets to a trustee, who oversees them based on the trust's conditions.

Tax Implications

Revocable Trusts: The assets put in a revocable trust are considered as part of your possessions for tax purposes, implying that they might incur estate taxes upon your death. Furthermore, any money generated by the trust will be subject to taxation under your name as the person who established it.

Irrevocable Trusts: When assets are moved into an irrevocable trust, they are excluded from your estate for estate tax purposes, since you no longer retain ownership of them. This could lead to substantial savings on taxes, particularly if the total value of your estate is higher than the federal estate tax exemption limit. Moreover, the trust itself is accountable for taking care of tax payments on any income it generates, which may be at a reduced rate based on the structure and nature of trust.

Asset Protection and Creditor Claims

Revocable Trusts: Provide limited protection from creditors during your lifetime since you retain ownership and control over the assets. Creditors have the right to pursue these assets as if they were still under your ownership.

Irrevocable Trusts: Offer significant asset protection by transferring ownership, ensuring your assets are safeguarded. Creditors cannot generally access these assets to satisfy claims against you. This makes irrevocable trusts a powerful tool for protecting your estate's value for future generations.

Suitability Based on Estate Planning Goals

Revocable Trusts: Best suited for individuals who desire flexibility and control over their assets while alive but still want to ensure a smooth transfer of these assets upon death, avoiding probate.

Irrevocable Trusts: This option is perfect for individuals who own substantial estates and wish to reduce estate taxes and shield assets from creditors. This strategy may involve relinquishing direct control over these assets in exchange for these protections.

Choosing between a revocable and irrevocable trust depends largely on your priorities, such as how much control you want to maintain, your tax planning needs, and your asset protection desires. Revocable trusts offer flexibility and control, making them suitable for most individuals, while irrevocable trusts provide strong protections and tax advantages, best suited for those with substantial assets and a clear, unchanging intent for their estate plan. By understanding the differences and implications of each type of trust, you can better align your estate planning strategy with your long-term goals, ensuring that your legacy is preserved according to your wishes.

Ways to Incorporate Some Flexibility into Irrevocable Trusts

Creating an irrevocable trust is a crucial aspect of estate planning, particularly useful for aspects like asset shielding, tax optimization, and wealth distribution. However, the inherent inflexibility of irrevocable trusts can be a concern. Once established, altering the terms or accessing the assets can be challenging. Despite this rigidity, there are several strategies to incorporate flexibility into an irrevocable trust, allowing for adaptability to changing circumstances and needs.

Using Trust Protectors

A practical method to introduce flexibility to an irrevocable trust is by designating a trust protector. Consider the trust protector as an impartial third party with specific powers outlined in the trust agreement. These powers can include the ability to amend the trust terms, change trustees, or modify beneficiary distributions in response to changing laws or circumstances. The role of the trust protector is to oversee the trust and ensure it achieves its intended goal, even as conditions evolve. By granting a trust protector the authority to make necessary adjustments, you introduce a layer of flexibility that can adapt to unforeseen changes.

Decanting the Trust

Decanting enables the trustee to move assets to a new trust with altered terms. This can be particularly useful when the original trust no longer serves its goal effectively due to evolutions in tax laws, beneficiary circumstances, or other factors. Decanting essentially "pours" the assets into a new trust, providing an opportunity to update the terms and add new provisions. However, decanting laws vary by state, so talking with an estate planning lawyer is key to grasp the particular regulations and restrictions in your jurisdiction.

Including a Power of Appointment

Incorporating a power of appointment into an irrevocable trust can provide significant flexibility. A power of appointment allows a designated individual, often the trust creator or a beneficiary, to direct how the trust assets are distributed, either during their lifetime or at their death. This power can be broad or limited, giving the holder discretion to adapt the trust's terms to meet changing needs and circumstances. By including a power of appointment, you enable adjustments to the trust with no need for formal amendments or court intervention.

Providing for Discretionary Distributions

Granting the trustee the authority to make discretionary distributions to beneficiaries can also add flexibility to an irrevocable trust. Discretionary distributions allow the trustee to respond to the beneficiaries' changing needs, such as educational expenses, medical costs, or financial hardships. This approach requires a high level of trust in the trustee's judgment and fiduciary duty, as they will have significant control over when and how trust assets are distributed. Clear guidelines and criteria for discretionary distributions should be outlined in the trust agreement to ensure the trustee acts in accordance with your intentions.

Using a Trust Amendment Clause

While an irrevocable trust cannot be easily amended, incorporating a specific amendment clause can provide a mechanism for future changes. This clause can grant the trustee or a trust protector the authority to amend the trust in certain circumstances, such as changes in tax laws or the beneficiary's needs. This approach requires precise drafting to ensure the amendment power is limited to appropriate situations and does not undermine the trust's overall purpose.

Section 15: Choosing Trustees

When to Put Yourself as Trustee and the Successor Trustee

When you're establishing a trust, a key choice you'll face is selecting the right trustees who will oversee it. This choice involves not just deciding who will manage your trust now, but also who will take over when you are no longer able to do so. Understanding the roles and making informed decisions about being your own trustee and appointing a successor are crucial for the smooth operation and long-term success of your trust.

The trustee wears many hats, overseeing the trust's assets, ensuring it follows your wishes, and always putting the beneficiaries' best interests first. This means you need to be meticulous in record-keeping, honest in handling assets, diligent in paying debts and taxes, and transparent in your dealings with beneficiaries. Whether you're managing investments, real estate, or other assets, you must maintain the highest level of integrity and efficiency.

When to Appoint Yourself as Trustee

Appointing yourself as trustee of your revocable living trust is a common and often practical choice, especially if you aim to keep control on your assets while you are alive. In this role, you manage your assets as if they were in your own name, but within the legal framework of the trust. This setup allows you to adjust the trust or move assets in and out of it with the flexibility you need to respond to changes in your life or financial situation.

When you appoint yourself as trustee, you enjoy several benefits. You have direct control over the management of your assets, which means you can make investment decisions, buy or sell property, and distribute assets to beneficiaries as you see fit. This arrangement also provides privacy and avoids the complications and delays of probate since the trust doesn't go through the court system after your death.

However, this role also requires you to plan for the future. It's crucial to consider what might happen if you're unable to make decisions for yourself or when you're no longer here. This is when the successor trustee steps in.

Choosing a Successor Trustee

The successor trustee has a critical part with regards to continuing the management of the trust after you can no longer do so. This transition can happen due to your incapacity or death, making it essential to choose someone who is reliable, capable, and ready to take over at a moment's notice.

Selecting the Right Person for the Job

The choice of successor trustee should be based on several key factors:

- Expertise: The individual must possess the requisite skills and knowledge, particularly if the trust contains complex assets or if there are tricky tax implications to manage.

- Impartiality: If your trust involves multiple beneficiaries who might have competing interests, it's key to select somebody that can act neutrally and fairly in managing the trust.

- Trustworthiness: The position needs someone who can be relied upon completely and who holds strong ethical principles, as they will be overseeing assets and making decisions that impact the financial futures of others.

- Availability and Willingness: Make sure the person you select is ready and wants to to take on the responsibilities of this role. Being a trustee can require a significant amount of time and can be quite challenging at times.

Common Choices

- Family Members: Many people choose a responsible family member because they are familiar with the family dynamics and understand the personal aspects of the trust. However, you should be cautious if this choice could lead to family conflict.

- Trusted Advisors: Attorneys, accountants, and financial advisors can make excellent trustees, especially if they have been involved in setting up the trust or have a long-standing professional relationship with you.

- Institutions: A bank or trust company can serve as a professional trustee, offering expertise and stability, particularly for larger trusts or when you want to ensure impartiality and professional management.

Working with Your Successor Trustee

To ensure a smooth transition, it's imperative to include your successor trustee in the trust management course as early as possible. They should understand the trust's structure, your vision for its operation, and the needs and personalities of your beneficiaries. Regular communication and joint decision-making can help prepare them for their eventual role, ensuring they are ready to take over when needed.

When Not to Be Your Own Trustee

There are situations where being your own trustee might not be the best option. If you have health issues that could lead to incapacity, or if managing the trust could become too burdensome due to the complexity of the assets or the dynamics of your family, it may be wise to consider appointing a co-trustee or successor trustee sooner rather than later.

Furthermore, if your trust is designed to support someone that needs special care or to safeguard assets from creditors, having an independent or professional trustee from the start can help to maintain the necessary legal safeguards and ensure the trust fulfills its purpose without complications.

Individual vs Corporate Trustees

The trustee's role is to administer the estate according to the trust document, and their responsibilities can be extensive and complex. Choosing an individual trustee often means selecting someone you know personally, like a member of your family, one of your friend, or professional counselor.

Pros of Choosing an Individual Trustee:

1. Personal Connection: An individual trustee often has a personal relationship with you and your family, which can make them more attuned to the specific needs and dynamics of your beneficiaries.

2. Flexibility: Individuals may offer more flexibility in managing the trust, able to make decisions quickly and adapt to changing circumstances without the red tape that can accompany corporate entities.

3. Cost: Generally, an individual trustee may be less expensive than a corporate trustee, as they might not charge a trustee fee or might charge a lower rate.

Cons of Choosing an Individual Trustee:

1. Potential for Bias: Their personal relationship with the family might lead to bias in decision-making or conflicts of interest.

2. Capacity and Expertise: An individual may lack the financial acumen or time needed to manage trust assets efficiently, especially if the trust is large or involves complex assets.

3. Continuity Concerns: Individuals may become ill, die, or become incapacitated, raising concerns about the ongoing management of the trust.

A corporate trustee usually refers to a bank or trust company that offers specialized services in managing trusts professionally.

Pros of Choosing a Corporate Trustee:

1. Professional Management: Corporate trustees have the expertise and resources to manage complex trusts and a variety of investment assets effectively.

2. Impartiality: A corporate trustee brings a level of impartiality to the table, ensuring decisions are guided solely by the trust's terms and what's best for the beneficiaries.

3. Continuity: A corporate trustee will not die or become incapacitated, providing continuity in administration over the lifetime of the trust, which can be particularly important for trusts intended to last multiple generations.

Cons of Choosing a Corporate Trustee:

1. Cost: Corporate trustees typically charge higher fees than individual trustees, which can include annual fees calculated as a fraction of the trust's value.

2. Less Personal: They may not have personal knowledge of the beneficiaries or the settlor's intentions beyond what is documented in the trust, which can sometimes result in decisions that might seem impersonal or less aligned with family nuances.

3. Rigidity: Corporate trustees may be less flexible, bound by company policies or more conservative in their investment or distribution approaches.

Making the Decision

When choosing between an individual and a corporate trustee, consider the following factors:

1. Size and Complexity of the Trust: Larger or more complex trusts may benefit from the expertise of a corporate trustee.

2. Personal vs. Financial Priorities: If personal understanding and family dynamics are critical, an individual trustee might be appropriate. If financial expertise and impartiality are paramount, a corporate trustee could be better.

3. Cost Considerations: Weigh the cost of professional management against the potential benefits in terms of asset growth and risk management.

4. Long-Term Security: Consider the long-term security and continuity of trust management, especially for trusts that are intended to last beyond your lifetime.

Choosing the right trustee is vital to ensure that your trust operates as intended, safeguarding your assets and caring for your beneficiaries according to your wishes. The decision to opt for an individual or a corporate trustee must be carefully aligned with your trust's stipulations and your personal needs and preferences. Always ensure that your choice aligns with your overall estate planning objectives and provides for the ongoing, effective management of the trust assets.

Identifying Ideal Characteristics in Trustees

Choosing the right trustee—whether an individual or a corporate entity—is pivotal for the effective management and execution of a trust. This chapter discusses the essential characteristics to consider when selecting both individual and corporate trustees, helping you make well-informed choices that match your estate planning objectives.

Characteristics of an Ideal Individual Trustee

An individual trustee typically manages the trust based on personal relationships with the grantor and beneficiaries. The role demands a blend of impartiality, reliability, and financial acumen. Key Characteristics to Look For:

1. Trustworthiness and Integrity: The foundation of a good trustee. This person will handle significant assets and make decisions that affect financial futures; hence, integrity is paramount.

2. Financial Acumen: Basic knowledge of financial management is crucial, especially for complex estates involving diverse assets like stocks, real estate, or businesses.

3. Availability and Commitment: Managing a trust is time-consuming. The selected person should be ready and willing to commit the required time and energy to carry out these responsibilities effectively.

4. Interpersonal Skills: A trustee needs superb communication abilities to engage with beneficiaries and mediate conflicts if they arise.

5. Understanding of Fiduciary Responsibilities: They must comprehend the legal responsibilities involved in managing a trust, including adhering to the trust's stipulations while prioritizing the beneficiaries' welfares.

6. Experience with Estate or Trust Management: While not mandatory, experience with financial management or estate planning is highly beneficial.

7. Impartiality: The ability to act fairly towards all beneficiaries, regardless of personal relationships.

Characteristics of an Ideal Corporate Trustee

Corporate trustees, like banks or trust companies, offer expert services in managing trusts. They offer expertise and continuity but at a higher cost. Key Characteristics to Look For:

1. Reputation and Reliability: A reputable corporate trustee is crucial for ensuring trust security. Seek firms with a proven history and high client satisfaction.

2. Expertise in Trust Management: Extensive experience in managing trusts similar to yours, with a comprehensive knowledge of applicable tax regulations and investment strategies.

3. Financial Stability: The corporate trustee should be financially robust to manage your assets securely over the long term.

4. Range of Services: They should offer comprehensive services that meet all your trust's needs, from tax planning to investment management.

5. Fee Structure: Make sure you grasp how the trustee fees are structured—whether they're based on a percentage of your assets, a flat rate, or a mix of both.

6. Accessibility and Customer Service: Good communication and service are essential. Ensure that you can easily get updates and make inquiries about your trust.

7. Flexibility and Personalization: Though typically less flexible than individuals, some corporate trustees might offer tailored services depending on your trust's complexity.

When you're assessing a corporate trustee, think about the following factors:

1. Consultations: Meet with several firms to discuss your trust needs and evaluate their proposals.

2. References and Reviews: Check client reviews and ask for references to gauge the firm's performance and client relationships.

3. Professional Advice: Engage an independent financial advisor to assess whether a corporate trustee's offerings align with your trust objectives.

Section 16: Frequent Issues to Avoid When Setting Up and Managing a Trust

Issues that could Arise when Setting Up the Trust

1. Lack of Clarity in Defining Trust Objectives

- Issue: Without clear goals, a trust may not serve its intended purpose, leading to mismanagement and beneficiary disputes.

- Prevention: Clearly define what you aim to achieve with your trust, whether it's asset protection, tax planning, or providing for loved ones, and communicate these goals to your attorney.

2. Choosing the Wrong Type of Trust

- Issue: Selecting an inappropriate type of trust can lead to increased taxes, inadequate asset protection, and unintended beneficiary disputes.

- Prevention: Talk to an estate planning expert to figure out which trust suits your needs. They will assist you decide based on what you own, your family's situation, and your personal goals.

3. Improper Funding of the Trust

- Issue: A trust must be properly funded with the correct titles transferred to the trust. If you don't do this, people might lose trust in you.

- Prevention: Work closely with legal and financial advisors to confirm all pertinent assets are properly transferred into the trust's name.

4. Neglecting to Choose the Right Trustee

- Issue: An ill-chosen trustee can lead to mismanagement of assets, conflicts of interest, or failure to comply with trust terms.

- Prevention: Select a trustee who is trustworthy, understands the family dynamics, and preferably has some financial acumen. Consider a corporate trustee if the estate is large or complex.

Issues that could Arise when Managing the Trust

1. Neglecting to Maintain Precise and Comprehensive Records

- Issue: Inadequate record-keeping can complicate tax filings and make it difficult to track the trust's performance.

- Prevention: Ensure that the trustee maintains detailed records of all transactions, distributions, and investment decisions.

2. Inadequate Communication with Beneficiaries

- Issue: Lack of regular communication can lead to misunderstandings or suspicions among beneficiaries, potentially resulting in legal challenges.

- Prevention: The trustee should provide regular updates to beneficiaries about the trust's status and decisions affecting their interests.

3. Not Adapting the Trust to Changed Circumstances

- Issue: As laws and family situations change, a trust that is not regularly reviewed may become outdated or ineffective.

- Prevention: Schedule regular reviews of the trust with legal advisors to adapt to changes in laws, family dynamics, or financial situations.

4. Ignoring Tax Implications

- Issue: Mismanagement of tax obligations can lead to unnecessary tax burdens or penalties.

- Prevention: The trustee should work with a tax expert to comprehend and handle the trust's tax implications efficiently.

Legal and Ethical Considerations

1. Breaching Fiduciary Duties

- Issue: Trustees who fail to serve the beneficiaries' best welfares risk legal action and can jeopardize the trust's integrity.

- Prevention: Trustees must understand their fiduciary duties and serve exclusively the beneficiaries' welfares, avoiding any conflicts of interest.

2. Not Using Discretion Wisely

- Issue: Trustees who fail to use their discretion appropriately when distributing assets can create inequities among beneficiaries.

- Prevention: Trustees should carefully consider the trust's terms and the settlor's intent when making discretionary decisions.

Section 17: Transferring Assets into The Trust

Guidelines to Transfer Real Estates

Why Transfer Real Estate into a Trust?

Putting your real estate into a trust can:

- Make sure your property goes directly to your beneficiaries without the hassle of probate.
- Provide continued management of the property if the grantor becomes incapacitated.
- Protect the property from potential lawsuits and creditors under certain conditions.

Step-by-Step Process for Transferring Real Estate into a Trust

Step 1: Identify the Property
- Select which real estate properties you want to place into the trust.
- Ensure that all documentation related to the property is current and accurate.

Step 2: Prepare the Deed

- Hire a real estate attorney or a qualified professional to draft a new deed transferring the property from your name into the name of the trust.

- The deed type will depend on your location and the specifics of the trust arrangement, commonly a quitclaim or warranty deed.

Step 3: Execute the Deed

- Sign the deed in the presence of a notary.

- Depending on the state, witness signatures may also be required.

Step 4: Record the Deed

- Record the deed at the local county recorder's office.

- Take care of any recording fees that may apply, as these can differ depending on where you are.

Legal Considerations, Potential Pitfalls and Issues

- Ensure that the transfer adheres to local and state real estate laws, which can vary widely.

- Think about how this might affect property taxes, transfer taxes, and the possibility of the property's value being reassessed.

- Make certain the trust document explicitly states the intention to include real estate as part of the trust's assets.

- Regularly review the trust's terms and funded assets to adapt to any changes in laws or personal circumstances.

- Errors in the deed or failure to properly record the document can lead to disputes or legal challenges.

- Understand how transferring real estate to a trust affects your tax obligations.

- Consult with a tax advisor to handle potential issues such as capital gains implications or the loss of homestead exemptions.

- If the property has a mortgage, inform the lender about the transfer to a trust.

- Review the mortgage agreement for any clauses that could complicate the transfer, such as due-on-sale clauses.

Financial Accounts Transfers

Integrating financial accounts into a trust is a smart move in estate planning. It helps to make sure that assets are managed and distributed more smoothly when the person who set up the trust is no longer able to do so or has passed away. The types of Financial Accounts typically Transferred into Trusts are:

- Bank accounts (checking and savings)

- Investment accounts (stocks, bonds, mutual funds)

- Retirement accounts (IRAs, 401(k)s, although these often require special considerations)

- Life insurance policies

Step-by-Step Process for Transferring Financial Accounts into a Trust

Step 1: Inventory Financial Accounts

- List all financial accounts you own and gather all related documentation, including account statements and ownership records.

Step 2: Consult Financial Institutions

- Reach out to each bank to find out what they need from you to move your accounts into a trust.

- Obtain any necessary forms or documents they require for the transfer process.

Step 3: Change Account Ownership

- Complete the necessary paperwork to transfer ownership of the accounts from your name to the name of the trust.

- This often involves providing a copy of the trust agreement and possibly a certification of trust that summarizes the trust's essential information without revealing private details.

Step 5: Verify and Update Beneficiary Designations

- If you have accounts like life insurance or retirement funds, make sure to update the beneficiary details to include your trust. This ensures that your estate planning goals are properly aligned.

Step 6: Confirm Transfer with Institutions

- After submitting all paperwork, follow up with financial institutions to confirm that the accounts have been successfully transferred into the trust.

- Obtain written confirmation or updated account statements for record-keeping.

Legal and Tax Considerations

- Ensure that all transfers adhere to federal and state laws, which can differ based on the type of account and the institution.

- Understand how transferring certain accounts can affect your tax situation, particularly with retirement accounts, which may have specific tax treatments when altered.

Common Pitfalls to Avoid

- Not involving your financial advisors or estate planners can lead to inconsistencies between your financial plan and estate plan.

- Unintended tax consequences can occur if transfers are not handled properly, especially with tax-deferred retirement accounts.

- Failing to properly complete the transfer process can result in accounts not being part of the trust, potentially leading to probate issues.

Transferring Other Personal Properties

Personal property encompasses a broad spectrum of tangible and intangible items such as:

- Furniture and home furnishings
- Art and collectibles
- Jewelry and personal items
- Vehicles

Including personal property in a trust simplifies the handling and allocation of these assets upon your death or incapacitation, provide privacy, and ensure that specific items are given to designated individuals according to your precise instructions.

Step-by-Step Process for Transferring Personal Property into a Trust

Step 1: Inventory Your Assets

- Catalog all personal property you intend to include in the trust. Detailed descriptions and appraisals may be necessary, especially for valuable items like art or antiques.

Step 2: Review Your Trust

- Ensure that your trust is set up to handle personal property. Some types of trusts may be more suitable for these assets than others, depending on your goals for control and distribution.

Step 3: Legally Transfer Ownership

- For tangible personal property, use a Bill of Sale or similar document to transfer ownership into the trust.
- For intangible assets like copyrights or patents, you may need to complete additional forms or registrations indicating the trust as the new owner.

Step 4: Document the Transfer

- Keep meticulous records of the transfer, including descriptions of the items, the method of transfer, and where the documentation is stored. This will be crucial for the trustee's management duties and for avoiding disputes among beneficiaries.

Step 5: Update Your Trust Document

- Amend your trust document or include a schedule of assets to specifically list personal property items covered by the trust.

Step 6: Communicate with Your Trustee and Beneficiaries

- Inform your trustee and beneficiaries about the inclusion of personal property in the trust, particularly if certain items have specific sentimental or monetary value. Clear communication can prevent misunderstandings and disputes.

Legal Considerations and Best Practices

- Depending on state laws, the transfer of certain assets into a trust may need to be witnessed or notarized to be legally binding.
- Regularly appraise high-value items to reflect accurate valuations in the trust documentation are vital for insurance considerations and equitable distribution.

- For items not specifically listed in the trust document, consider attaching a personal property memorandum that can be updated without formal amendments to the trust itself.

Common Pitfalls to Avoid

- Without proper documentation, proving an item's intended purpose was to be part of the trust can be hard, leading to potential legal challenges.

- As you acquire new personal property or circumstances change, regularly updating the trust is essential to include or remove items as necessary.

- Although personal property is not typically a significant concern for estate taxes, it is crucial to think about potential state taxes or the impacts for high-value collections.

Transferring Investment and Business Interests

Effectively incorporating investment and business interests into a trust is a sophisticated aspect of estate planning. Investment and business interests range from stocks and bonds to partial or whole ownership in private or public companies. Transferring these assets into a trust involves not only legal considerations but also strategic planning to ensure continuity, minimize tax liabilities, and protect the assets from personal creditors.

Step-by-Step Process for Transferring Investment and Business Interests

Step 1: Review Your Assets

- Inventory your investments and business interests. Detail every asset, including stock holdings, bonds, mutual funds, business entities, and other relevant investments.

- Assess the implications of transferring each asset. Consider tax implications, the impact on business operations, and your future financial needs.

Step 2: Establish or Amend the Trust

- Pick the correct type of trust. Depending on your goals—whether it's maintaining control over the business or ensuring financial support for your family—a revocable or irrevocable trust might be more suitable.

- Talk with an estate lawyer to draft or adjust your trust document to include precise provisions for handling business and investment assets.

Step 3: Valuation of Assets

- Obtain a current valuation of all business interests and significant investments. Accurate valuations are crucial for fair distribution, tax assessments, and future trust management.

- Engage with experts like certified public accountants (CPAs) or valuation experts, especially for private business interests.

Step 4: Transfer Ownership

- Prepare and execute transfer documents. For stocks and bonds, this might involve working with a broker or financial institution to retitle accounts. For business interests, you may need to collaborate with a business counsellor in order to be in compliance with corporate laws.

- Record changes in ownership at the appropriate registries or with transfer agents, ensuring that all paperwork reflects the trust as the new owner.

Step 5: Update Business Agreements

- Review and amend business agreements as necessary. This includes buy-sell agreements, shareholder agreements, or operating agreements to accommodate the trust as a new business entity owner.

- Notify business partners and stakeholders of the change in ownership to maintain transparency and operational continuity.

Step 6: Manage Tax Implications

- Talk to a tax advisor so you can fully grasp and handle the tax consequences involved when moving your assets into a trust.

-This includes addressing potential capital gains taxes, estate taxes, and gift taxes.

- Plan for ongoing tax obligations of the trust, which might differ significantly from personal tax obligations, especially if the trust generates income.

Legal and Ethical Considerations and Common Pitfalls

- Ensure that all transfers adhere to securities regulations and corporate laws, particularly for publicly traded instruments or when modifying corporate ownership structures.

- The trustee's fiduciary duty includes managing these assets prudently and in the best interest of the beneficiaries. Selecting a trustee who is capable of understanding and managing complex assets is critical.

- Ensure the trust has enough liquidity to handle obligations like taxes, distributions, or operational needs without requiring the premature sale of valuable assets.

- Consider how changes in ownership might affect business operations, employee morale, and external business relationships.

- Regularly reviewing your situation is crucial to stay responsive to market shifts, changes in tax laws, and your personal circumstances.

Transfer of Intellectual Property

Intellectual Property (IP) is a key asset class that can include everything from patents and trademarks to copyrights, designs, and trade secrets. Placing these assets in a trust can help safeguard and manage them more effectively, ensuring they contribute to your estate's value and your beneficiaries' welfare.

Intellectual Property encompasses human creations like inventions, artistic works, designs, and commercial symbols, names, and images.

IP is safeguarded by legal means such as patents, copyrights, trademarks, and similar protections. These laws enable individuals to gain recognition and financial rewards for their creative endeavors.

Why Transfer IP into a Trust?

- Asset Protection: A trust can provide a protective shield for IP assets against creditors and litigants.

- Estate Planning: Including IP in your trust helps ensure these assets are conveyed smoothly to your beneficiaries bypassing the complexities of probate.

- Tax Benefits: When correctly established, a trust can reduce estate and gift taxes associated with high-value IP assets.

- Control and Management: A trust can ensure professional management and licensing of IP, potentially providing ongoing income for beneficiaries.

Step-by-Step Process for Transferring IP into a Trust

Step 1: Inventory Your Intellectual Property

- List Your IP Assets: Include all patents, copyrights, trademarks, domain names, and any other IP rights.

- Value Your IP: Assess the current market value of your IP. This may require a professional valuation, especially for patents or copyrights with significant commercial use.

Step 2: Establish or Review Your Trust

- Type of Trust: Decide if a revocable or irrevocable trust is best suited for your IP assets, based on your control and flexibility needs.

- Trust Terms: Make sure the legal document clearly states that intellectual property can be included, and specifies how these assets should be handled and distributed.

Step 3: Transfer Ownership

- Legal Documentation: Prepare the necessary transfer documents. This typically involves 'assignment agreements' that transfer your ownership rights in the IP to the trust.

- Record the Transfer: For registered IP like patents and trademarks, file the necessary forms with the relevant government bodies (e.g., the U.S. Patent and Trademark Office) to record the trust as the new owner.

Step 4: Manage Tax Implications

- Understand Tax Consequences: Transferring IP into a trust can cause various tax implications, including profit from asset sales or gift taxes. Make sure to consult a tax advisor to guide you through these matters.

- File Necessary Returns: Ensure that any required tax returns are filed, including gift tax returns if the transfer into the trust is considered a gift.

Step 5: Communicate with Stakeholders

- Inform Beneficiaries: Make sure beneficiaries understand the value and potential income from the IP assets.

- Update Business Agreements: If your IP is licensed or involved in business agreements, update these contracts to reflect the trust as the new owner.

Legal Considerations and Challenges

- Different types of IP are governed by different rules. For instance, copyrights are automatically in place upon creation, while patents require a rigorous application process.

- Ensure that all IP assets are properly registered and protected before transferring them into a trust.

- IP can be a uniquely challenging asset to value and manage due to its often subjective and fluctuating worth.

- Regular re-evaluation of the IP assets and professional management is recommended to maximize their value within the trust.

- IP transfers must be meticulously documented to ensure legal standing. Neglecting this can lead to disputes or loss of rights.

- Ensure all transfer paperwork is detailed, precise, and legally binding.

- Many IP assets require ongoing actions to maintain their legal protection, such as patent renewals or copyright registrations.

- The trustee needs to be aware of and manage these requirements to prevent the unintentional loss of IP rights.

- If your IP has registrations in multiple countries, be aware that different jurisdictions have different rules for trusts and IP rights.

- Consult with legal experts in relevant countries to ensure your trust's structure and the IP transfer comply with local laws.

Moving Life Insurance

Incorporating life insurance into a trust is a strategic move in estate planning, offering benefits like enhanced financial security for beneficiaries and potential tax advantages. First, let's break down the different types of life insurance policies so we can understand them better:

1. Term Life Insurance: It offers consistent financial protection for a specific period, like 10, 20, or 30 years, with fixed premium payments.

2. Whole Life Insurance: Offers coverage for the insured's entire lifetime, accumulating a cash value that can be withdrawn or borrowed against.

3. Universal Life Insurance: Offers low-cost protection as the term life insurance and a savings element.

Benefits of Transferring Life Insurance into a Trust

1. Avoidance of Probate: Registering a life insurance policy in a trust ensures the death benefit is directly paid to the trust, bypassing the probate process and ensuring faster access to funds by beneficiaries.

2. Estate Tax Benefits: Keeping the life insurance separate from the insured's estate can significantly lower estate taxes, based on the total estate value and existing tax laws threshold.

3. Control Over the Distribution: A trust can specify how, when, and under what conditions beneficiaries receive the death benefit, providing structured support according to the grantor's wishes.

4. Asset Protection: Trusts can offer protection against creditors and divorce settlements, ensuring that the proceeds go to the intended beneficiaries.

Step-by-Step Process for Transferring Life Insurance into a Trust

Step 1: Establish the Trust

- Choose the Type of Trust: Typically, an Irrevocable Life Insurance Trust (ILIT) is used for this purpose because it removes the policy from the insured's estate. Potentially work with an estate planning professional to create the trust document, specifying trustees, beneficiaries, and terms of asset management and distribution.

Step 2: Transfer Ownership of the Policy

- Existing Policies: Change the owner of the life insurance policy to the trust by completing a change of ownership form provided by the insurance carrier or by assigning the trust as beneficiary.

- New Policies: If purchasing a new policy, the trust should be established first, and then the policy should be purchased directly by the trustee of the trust.

Step 3: Notify the Insurance Company

- Submit Required Documents: Provide the insurance company with a copy of the trust agreement and any other required documentation to confirm the change of ownership.

- Confirm the Change: Ensure that the insurance company records the trust as the new policy owner and, if desired, as the beneficiary.

Step 4: Pay Premiums Through the Trust

- Fund the Trust: Ensure the trust has enough funds to continue paying the premiums on the life insurance policy. This can be done by transferring funds to the trust or by the grantor making annual gifts to the trust.

- Maintain Records: Keep detailed records of premium payments to ensure they are made on time and from the correct accounts to maintain the policy's validity.

Legal and Tax Considerations

- Gift Tax Issues: If the trust pays the premiums, these payments are considered gifts to the beneficiaries and may require the filing of gift tax if they surpass the annual exclusion limit.

- Three-Year Rule: If an existing policy is transferred into a trust and the insured dies within three years, the IRS can still consider the insurance proceeds part of the estate for estate tax purposes.

- Managing the Policy: The trustee must ensure that the policy remains in force and is managed according to the trust terms.

- Communicating with Beneficiaries: Trustees should regularly update beneficiaries about the policy details and clarify how they will receive any benefits.

- Regular Review: Life insurance policies and the corresponding trust terms should be reviewed regularly to adapt to changes in tax laws, financial situations, and family dynamics.

- Proper Documentation: Ensure that all paperwork is correctly executed when transferring ownership to avoid unintended tax consequences or disputes.

- Sufficient Funding: The trust must be adequately funded to maintain the policy; otherwise, the policy could lapse, leaving beneficiaries without the intended benefits.

Section 18: Setting Conditional Releasing in Trusts

Setting conditional releases in a trust is a good way to make sure that the assets you leave behind are utilized in manners consistent with your principles and intentions. This approach allows you to specify conditions under which beneficiaries can access funds, encouraging responsible behavior and supporting their personal and professional growth. Here we explore various scenarios where conditional releases can be applied, including their descriptions, appropriate uses, and key benefits.

For Education

Conditional releases for education are designed to provide beneficiaries with funds specifically for educational purposes. This can cover tuition fees, living expenses while studying, books, and other educational supplies. The trust can be structured to release funds directly to the educational institution or to the beneficiary, provided they submit proof of enrollment and good academic standing.

When to Use It

This condition is used when you want to prioritize education in your beneficiaries' lives. It is particularly useful for:

- Ensuring that funds are available throughout the beneficiaries' educational journey, from primary school up to higher education.

- Encouraging beneficiaries to pursue further education, such as college degrees or vocational training, without financial stress.

Key Benefits

- Encourages Education: Ensures that recipients receive the financial assistance necessary to successfully finish their education, supporting their academic journey.

- Reduces Misuse: Reduces the chances of money being used for purposes other than originally intended.

- Supports Long-Term Success: By prioritizing education, beneficiaries are more likely to secure a solid foundation for future career success.

For Healthcare

Conditional releases for healthcare allow beneficiaries to access funds for medical expenses, including emergency treatment, routine check-ups, mental health services, and long-term medical care. This ensures that beneficiaries' health and well-being are maintained without the burden of large medical bills.

When to Use It

Employ this clause to ensure that beneficiaries can receive excellent healthcare without worrying about financial barriers. It is especially important:

- For beneficiaries with known health issues who will require continuous medical care.

- When you wish to provide a safety net that covers unexpected medical expenses.

Key Benefits

- Promotes Well-Being: Promotes the overall well-being, both physically and mentally, of those it serves.

- Financial Security: Prevents significant medical bills from disrupting the beneficiaries' financial stability.

- Comprehensive Support: Can be tailored to cover a wide range of healthcare services, ensuring beneficiaries receive the care they need when they need it.

For First Home Purchase

This conditional release makes funds available for beneficiaries to purchase their first home. This can significantly reduce the financial barriers to homeownership, providing a stable living situation and an investment in the beneficiaries' future.

When to Use It

This is ideal for helping beneficiaries establish themselves and start building equity. It's particularly beneficial:

- When beneficiaries are at a stage where they are starting their own families or looking to move out independently.

- To encourage financial responsibility and planning.

Key Benefits

- Facilitates Homeownership: Helps beneficiaries overcome the often prohibitive cost of buying a first home.

- Builds Equity: Helps beneficiaries invest in something that grows in value over the years, benefiting them in the long run.

- Promotes Independence: Encourages beneficiaries to take a significant step towards financial and personal independence.

For Travel and Cultural Experience

Funds released for travel and cultural experiences are intended to broaden the beneficiaries' horizons. This can include gap years, educational tours, cultural exchange programs, or personal travel that fosters learning and personal growth.

When to Use It

This condition is ideal for promoting personal development and global awareness. It is particularly useful:

- For young adults or students who can benefit from exposure to different cultures and global perspectives.

- When you value travel as a means of education and personal growth.

Key Benefits

- Encourages Exploration: Enables beneficiaries to discover the world, acquire new languages, and immerse themselves in diverse cultures.

- Personal Development: Travel has the power to profoundly change us, fostering personal growth, independence, and a wider view of the world.

- Educational Value: Many travel experiences have an educational component that can complement formal education.

For Creating a Company

This condition supports beneficiaries who wish to start their own business by providing initial capital. It encourages entrepreneurial spirit by offering financial support for start-up costs, business planning, and initial operations.

When to Use It

Ideal for beneficiaries with a strong entrepreneurial drive and a viable business idea. It's particularly beneficial:

- When you want to support job creation and economic growth.
- To encourage beneficiaries to develop business skills and self-reliance.

Key Benefits

- Fosters Entrepreneurship: Provides the financial resources needed to start and grow a new business.
- Promotes Self-Sufficiency: Encourages beneficiaries to develop and rely on their own skills and talents.
- Economic Impact: By backing new businesses, you are crucial in driving economic growth and generating employment opportunities on a larger scale.

For Life Milestones

Trusts can release funds to celebrate or support significant life milestones such as weddings, the birth of children, or the achievement of major life goals. These releases can help cover expenses associated with these events or provide a financial boost at critical moments.

When to Use It

This is useful when you want to ensure that beneficiaries have support during key life events. It's especially appropriate:

- For providing a gift or inheritance that acknowledges significant personal achievements or transitions.
- To help beneficiaries manage the costs associated with important life stages, such as marriage or the arrival of a child.

Key Benefits

- Supports Key Transitions: Helps beneficiaries financially during important life changes.
- Celebrates Achievements: Provides a way to celebrate and acknowledge major life milestones.
- Enhances Life Quality: Helps cover costs that can improve the overall standard of living for beneficiaries.

Limitation on Withdrawal

Setting limitations on withdrawals helps ensure that beneficiaries do not deplete their trust funds prematurely. These limitations can be structured as caps on the amount that can be withdrawn annually or restrictions based on specific criteria.

When to Use It

This approach is necessary when you want to protect the long-term financial security of the beneficiaries by preventing reckless spending. It's beneficial:

- For beneficiaries who might lack the know-how or self-control to handle significant amounts of money prudently.

- To provide a steady income over time, rather than allowing the trust fund to be quickly exhausted.

Key Benefits

- Encourages Financial Discipline: Teaches beneficiaries to plan and budget rather than spending impulsively.

- Protects Financial Security: Ensures that the trust assets last longer, providing financial security over a more extended period.

- Reduces Risk of Mismanagement: Minimizes the likelihood of financial mismanagement and the negative consequences that can follow.

Age-Based Distribution

Age-based distribution refers to the process of releasing funds when the recipient reaches specific age milestones. It ensures that financial support aligns with the beneficiary's life stages. This staggered approach can be set to coincide with stages in life where financial support can be most beneficial, like completing education, starting a career, or buying a home.

When to Use It

This is effective for providing financial support that aligns with the beneficiary's life stages. It's ideal:

- To introduce younger beneficiaries gradually to larger sums of money, allowing them to grow into their financial responsibilities.

- When you want to ensure that the inheritance supports the beneficiary at multiple stages of their development.

Key Benefits

- Supports Development: Matches financial support with the beneficiary's developmental and life stages.

- Teaches Money Management: Allows beneficiaries to learn to manage smaller amounts before accessing more significant funds.

- Provides Timely Support: Ensures that beneficiaries receive financial support when it can be most beneficial for their personal and professional growth.

Incentive Provisions

Incentive provisions are clauses in a trust that release funds when beneficiaries achieve specific goals or demonstrate certain behaviors. These goals can be educational achievements, maintaining steady employment, or other personal and professional milestones.

When to Use It

Use incentive provisions to motivate beneficiaries towards positive behaviors and accomplishments. They are particularly effective:

- To encourage hard work, perseverance, and responsible behavior.
- When you want to link financial rewards with personal effort and achievement.

Key Benefits

- Motivates Positive Behavior: Encourages beneficiaries to strive towards goals that you value.
- Rewards Achievement: Provides a tangible reward for achieving significant milestones.
- Aligns Financial Benefits with Personal Growth: Ensures that financial gains are aligned with personal and professional development.

Section 19: Exploring Different Categories of Trusts and Their Uses

1. Testamentary Trusts

Description

A Testamentary Trust is set up through a will and only becomes active after the person who created it passes away. This type of trust is part of the will, meaning it goes through the probate process. It allows a grantor to control asset distribution to beneficiaries under specific conditions set out in the will. Often used to provide for minors, manage estate taxes, or support a surviving spouse, it ensures assets are distributed in a structured manner.

Use Case(s)/When to Use

Perfect for safeguarding beneficiaries who might struggle with handling their inheritance because of their age, a disability, or lack of financial experience. It's especially useful for providing for minors, disabled family members, or protecting assets from beneficiaries' creditors.

Who Should Be the Trustee

Typically, the executor of the will acts as the trustee, but the grantor can designate any trusted individual or institution to manage the managing the trust's possessions in line with the will's instructions.

Type

Irrevocable — It takes effect and cannot be changed once the grantor passes away.

Key Benefits

- Makes sure that the assets are handled and shared in the way the grantor intended.
- Provides financial management and support to minors or beneficiaries with special needs.
- It can be structured to optimize estate taxes and defend assets from the creditors of the beneficiaries.

When It Is Created

It is created at the grantor's death and outlined in the grantor's last will.

Tax Implications

Assets go through probate, but with good preparation, you can optimize the tax impact. Beneficiaries receive distributions that might be subject to income tax depending on the nature of the distribution.

Control Over Assets

The trustee controls the assets and manages distributions as per the will's instructions.

Duration

Can last until a specified event occurs (like a beneficiary reaching a certain age) or for the beneficiaries' lifetimes.

Asset Protection

Offers protection from creditors for the beneficiaries, especially when distributions are discretionary.

Eligibility Requirements

Beneficiaries are defined by the grantor in the will. No specific eligibility requirements for establishing the trust, other than creating a valid will.

Favorable Jurisdictions

All U.S. states allow testamentary trusts, but specifics can vary by state. States with favorable trust laws include Delaware, Nevada, and South Dakota due to their privacy laws and tax advantages.

Other Considerations

It requires going through probate, which might cause delays and increase expenses. Careful drafting is required to make sure that the trust's terms are as intended by the grantor.

Challenges & Limitations

- The details become public records as part of the probate process.

- Managing the trust can be complex, requiring a knowledgeable trustee, especially for long-term distributions.

Example

A father could use a testamentary trust within the will to make sure that their children are financially supported for education and living expenses until they reach adulthood, at which point they might receive a lump sum or continue to receive managed distributions.

2. Spousal Lifetime Access Trusts (SLATs)

Description

A Spousal Lifetime Access Trust (SLAT) is a permanent trust where one spouse transfers assets to benefit the other spouse. This allows the donor spouse to use their gift tax exemption while providing financial benefits to the beneficiary spouse without the transferred assets being included in either spouse's estate, thereby reducing potential estate taxes.

Use Case(s)/When to Use

Used by married couples to optimize estate taxes and provide financial security for the beneficiary spouse without giving up access to the assets for family needs. It's effective for wealthy individuals aiming to utilize tax exemptions and safeguard assets from future creditors.

Who Should Be the Trustee

An independent trustee is recommended to ensure the trust complies with legal requirements for tax purposes and to manage the trust impartially.

Type

Irrevocable — This ensures the assets moved into the SLAT are permanently out of the donor's estate.

Key Benefits

- Provides a steady stream of benefits to the beneficiary spouse while minimizing estate taxes.

- Assets inside the SLAT are well protected from legal claims and creditors.

- Allows significant estate and gift tax planning opportunities, utilizing exemptions effectively.

When It Is Created

During the donor spouse's lifetime, enabling the couple to benefit from immediate tax advantages and asset protection.

Tax Implications

Assets transferred to the trust use the donor's lifetime gift tax exemption and are not considered part of the donor's estate in order to calculate estate taxes. Distributions to the beneficiary spouse are typically tax-free.

Control Over Assets

The trustee controls the trust assets but must adhere to the trust terms, which generally include providing for the beneficiary spouse's needs.

Duration

The SLAT can last for the beneficiary spouse's lifetime, and then benefit other family members like children or grandchildren.

Asset Protection

High — The trust assets are generally protected from both spouses' creditors, particularly if an independent trustee manages the trust.

Eligibility Requirements

The donor and beneficiary must be married at the time the SLAT is established. Trust provisions must be carefully structured to avoid unintended tax consequences.

Favorable Jurisdictions

States like Nevada, Delaware, and Alaska are preferred due to favorable trust and tax laws, privacy provisions, and innovative legal structures.

Other Considerations

Requires careful planning to avoid negative tax consequences, particularly in ensuring that the SLAT does not violate the reciprocal trust doctrine, which can happen if both spouses create similar trusts for each other.

Challenges & Limitations

- If not properly structured, could be subject to scrutiny under the reciprocal trust doctrine.
- Irrevocability means the donor spouse cannot reclaim gifted assets.

Example

A wealthy couple might establish a SLAT allowing the donor spouse to place $10 million into the trust, using their gift tax exemption while ensuring the beneficiary spouse has access to trust income and principal under certain conditions to maintain lifestyle and help with family expenses.

3. Marital Trusts / "A" Trusts

Description

Marital Trusts, or "A" Trusts, are intended to offer advantages to the surviving spouse and are part of an A-B trust arrangement to maximize estate tax efficiency. The trust holds assets for the surviving partner's benefit, with the rest of the possessions ultimately going to other beneficiaries, often being the children. These trusts take advantage of the unlimited marital deduction to postpone estate taxes until after the death of the surviving spouse.

Use Case(s)/When to Use

These are used to offer financial assistance to the surviving spouse without immediately incurring estate taxes and to ensure that the remaining assets eventually pass to other beneficiaries in a tax-efficient manner. Ideal for couples looking to maximize the use of their marital deductions while planning for the next generation.

Who Should Be the Trustee

Often, the surviving spouse is named as the trustee, which allows them direct control over the trust assets to meet their living needs. Alternatively, an independent trustee can be appointed for greater oversight and asset management.

Type

Irrevocable — The trust terms are set upon the death of the first spouse, as per the couple's estate plan.

Key Benefits

- It enables allowing the surviving spouse to access the trust's assets without immediate estate taxation obligations, postponing these taxes until their own passing.

- Provides a structured method to transfer wealth to the next generation while ensuring the surviving spouse's well-being.

- Utilizes the unlimited marital deduction to avoid estate taxes on the first spouse's death.

When It Is Created

At the first spouse's death, under the terms laid out in the deceased spouse's estate plan.

Tax Implications

Assets within the trust are included in the surviving spouse's estate when they pass away, resulting in them being liable for estate taxes. However, they are not taxed when the first spouse dies, thanks to the marital deduction.

Control Over Assets

If the surviving spouse is the trustee, they have significant control over the trust's income and, depending on the trust terms, potentially the principal. If an independent trustee is appointed, their control is guided by the trust terms.

Duration

Lasts until the surviving partner's death, after that the remaining assets are distributed to other beneficiaries as specified by the trust.

Asset Protection

Moderate — The trust can offer protection from creditors, especially if provisions limit the surviving spouse's access to the principal.

Eligibility Requirements

The primary beneficiary must be the surviving partner, usually required to be a United States citizen to fully utilize the marital deduction without additional tax obligations.

Favorable Jurisdictions

Generally recognized in all U.S. states, but jurisdictions like Delaware and South Dakota provide additional benefits in terms of privacy and flexible trust laws.

Other Considerations

- Careful drafting is required to ensure the trust meets the requirements for the marital deduction.

- Preparation should contemplate the potential for remarriage or changes in the surviving spouse's financial needs.

Challenges & Limitations

- The need to balance the provisions for surviving partner while also safeguarding also some resources for other beneficiaries.

- Potential complications with state-specific marital laws and elective share rights.

Example

In the case of a couple where one spouse deceases leaving $7 mln in assets. By transferring these assets into a Marital Trust, the surviving partner can access and benefit from the trust assets, receiving income, while the residual assets transfer to the successors while optimizing taxes after the spouse's passing.

Key Differences Between A-Trusts and SLATs

While both A-Trusts and SLATs are designed to provide for a surviving or beneficiary spouse, they have distinct differences that can impact estate planning decisions:

Timing and Control

A-Trust: Set up at the first spouse's death as part of the AB Trust strategy.

SLAT: Established during the spouses' lifetimes and is irrevocable from the start.

Tax Implications

A-Trust: Utilizes the marital deduction to defer estate taxes on assets until the surviving spouse's death.

SLAT: Uses the donor spouse's lifetime gift tax exemption to remove assets from the estate immediately, avoiding future estate taxes on the appreciation of these assets.

Access to Assets

A-Trust: The spouse who survives typically has full access to the money the trust earns, and depending on the trust's rules, they might also be able to use the savings itself.

SLAT: The beneficiary spouse's access to the trust's assets and income is determined by the trust's terms set at its creation, which can range from very restrictive to relatively liberal, depending on the goals.

Estate Inclusion

A-Trust: Assets in the A-Trust are included in the surviving spouse's estate unless they are spent down during their lifetime.

SLAT: Assets in the SLAT, and their growth, are generally excluded from both spouses' estates if structured correctly.

Protection from Creditors

A-Trust: Offers some level of creditor protection, this will depend on state laws and the trust's structure.

SLAT: Typically offers robust protection from creditors due to its irrevocable nature.

4. A-B Trusts

Description

A-B Trusts are designed to split a deceased spouse's estate into two parts to maximize estate tax exemptions and efficiently manage estate taxes. The "A" Trust, or Marital Trust, benefits the surviving spouse by securing their financial support and potentially principal from the estate. The "B" Trust, also sometimes referred as a Bypass Trust, is created to safeguard assets equivalent to the estate tax exemption. Its purpose is to benefit other beneficiaries besides the surviving spouse, ensuring these assets are excluded from the taxable estate of the surviving spouse.

Use Case(s)/When to Use

This trust structure is used by married partners who wish to ensure financial security for the surviving spouse and maintain the estate tax exemption for assets meant to pass to children or other beneficiaries. It is particularly effective in managing estate taxes for larger estates and guaranteeing that assets are secured and transferred in alignement to the couple's wishes.

Who Should Be the Trustee

For the A Trust, the surviving spouse often serves as the trustee, which allows them direct access to the trust's income and principal, as needed. For the B Trust, an independent trustee — such as a trusted advisor or institution — is recommended to manage the assets and protect the intended beneficiaries' interests.

Type

Irrevocable — The structure becomes irrevocable upon the death of the first spouse.

Key Benefits

- Allows for full use of both spouses' estate tax exemptions, potentially doubling the amount protected from estate taxes.

- Provides income and support to the surviving spouse from the A Trust.

- Preserves assets for future generations in the B Trust without additional estate taxes after the passing of the surviving partner.

When It Is Created

At the death of the first spouse, as specified in the estate planning documents of the deceased.

Tax Implications

- The A Trust can take advantage of the unlimited marital deduction, which means that estate taxes are postponed till the surviving partner deceases.

- The B Trust are protected from estate taxes when the surviving partner dies, thanks to the tax exemption applied to the deceased's estate.

Control Over Assets

The surviving spouse can control the A Trust assets. The B Trust is controlled by the trustee and is designed to benefit other heirs while minimizing their future estate tax burden.

Duration

The A Trust typically lasts till the death of the surviving spouse. The B Trust can continue according to the terms set out for the beneficiaries, often children or grandchildren.

Asset Protection

- A Trust provides moderate protection, depending on the access given to the living spouse.

- B Trust offers high protection from creditors and preserves assets for future generations.

Eligibility Requirements

Spouses need to structure their estate planning documents to create A-B Trusts, with beneficiaries typically being the couple's children or other heirs.

Favorable Jurisdictions

Jurisdictions like Delaware, South Dakota, and Nevada offer favorable laws for A-B Trusts due to privacy and favorable tax laws.

Other Considerations

- The trusts need to be meticulously organized to meet IRS regulations in order to gain the intended tax advantages, ensuring everything is set up correctly.

- Proper administration post-first spouse's death is crucial to maintain the benefits of the A-B structure.

Challenges & Limitations

- The irrevocable nature means decisions must be well-planned.

- Complexity in managing two trusts can increase administrative costs and oversight requirements.

Example

A couple with an estate of $20 million can use an A-B Trust structure to ensure that when one spouse dies, $10 million (assuming this is below the estate tax exemption threshold) is put in the B Trust, protecting it from estate taxes at the surviving spouse's later death, while the remaining $10 million is placed in the A Trust to provide for the surviving spouse.

5. Qualified Terminable Interest Property Trusts (QTIP)

Description

A Qualified Terminable Interest Property (QTIP) Trust enables one spouse to support the other spouse during their lifetime while retaining authority over the administration of the trust's assets after the surviving partner deceases. This is particularly useful in blended families or in cases of doubts about the ultimate distribution of the estate. The surviving partner receives proceeds from the trust, and the grantor specifies who the final beneficiaries of the residual assets will be subsequently the last spouse's death.

Use Case(s)/When to Use

QTIP Trusts are used to support a surviving spouse though ensuring eventual asset transfer to the children from a previous marriage or other specific beneficiaries. This allows the grantor to protect the interests of their chosen heirs while still supporting their spouse.

Who Should Be the Trustee

An independent trustee is often chosen to ensure impartial administration and adherence to the trust terms, especially important in blended family situations.

Type

Irrevocable — The trust's terms are set and cannot be changed after the grantor's death.

Key Benefits

- Provides income and potentially the initial capital to the surviving spouse while not granting them authority over the ultimate distribution of the assets.

- Makes sure that assets are ultimately transferred to the grantor's selected beneficiaries, not just those chosen by the surviving spouse.

- Allows the estate to be eligible for the marital deduction while still controlling asset distribution.

When It Is Created

At the grantor's death, as specified in their estate plan.

Tax Implications

The assets held in the QTIP Trust can benefit from the marital deduction while the surviving spouse is alive, delaying estate taxes till the surviving partner's death. At that point, these assets become part of their taxable estate.

Control Over Assets

The trustee controls the assets but must provide for the surviving spouse according to the trust terms. The surviving spouse does not control the disposition of the assets after their death.

Duration

Lasts until the death of the surviving spouse, after which the assets are distributed to the remainder beneficiaries.

Asset Protection

Moderate — The trust can safeguard the assets from the surviving partner's creditors and any irresponsible spending.

Eligibility Requirements

The surviving spouse must be entitled to receive all the income from the trust, payable annually. The ultimate beneficiaries are typically specified by the grantor.

Favorable Jurisdictions

All states recognize QTIP Trusts under federal law, but states like Delaware and South Dakota offer advantages in privacy and flexible trust structures.

Other Considerations

- Requires careful drafting to ensure the QTIP election qualifies for the marital deduction.

- Can be a point of contention in blended families if not communicated properly.

Challenges & Limitations

- Balancing the surviving spouse's needs with the intended final beneficiaries can be complex.

- The full inclusion of the trust assets within the estate of the surviving spouse might lead to a bigger amount in estate taxes to be paid than initially planned.

Example

A husband in a second marriage establishes a QTIP Trust to support his new wife from his $15 million estate. The trust stipulates that his wife will receive income for life, but upon her death, the principal goes to his children from his first marriage, ensuring his children inherit the majority of his wealth.

6. Special Needs Trusts

Description

Special Needs Trusts (SNTs) are created to offer economic assistance to people that need special care while ensuring they can still receive crucial government benefits like Medicaid or Supplemental Security Income (SSI). These trusts fund supplementary expenses (like caregiving, medical equipment, personal care items) that public assistance doesn't cover, without affecting the beneficiary's eligibility for those benefits.

Use Case(s)/When to Use

SNTs are crucial for beneficiaries who receive government assistance based on their financial need. They ensure that an inheritance or gift doesn't disqualify them from these advantages by offering funds that enhance without substituting government aid.

Who Should Be the Trustee

Choosing a trustee who understands the beneficiary's needs and the complexities of government programs is essential. This can be a family member with support from legal advisors or a professional trustee with experience in special needs planning.

Type

Irrevocable — To ensure the beneficiary does not have direct access or control that could impact their benefit eligibility.

Key Benefits

- Maintains the beneficiary's eligibility for public assistance benefits.

- Provides for additional care and services over the beneficiary's lifetime that enhances their quality of life.

- Offers a structured way to leave assets to a loved one with special needs without risking their essential public benefits.

When It Is Created

Can be established at any time but often is set up by parents or guardians as part of their estate planning.

Tax Implications

Contributions to the trust do not typically provide tax benefits to the donor but ensure the assets are managed in a tax-efficient way for the beneficiary.

Control Over Assets

The trustee has complete authority to decide how money is spent, ensuring it benefits the individual with special needs without replacing government aid.

Duration

Usually, these trusts last for the lifetime of the beneficiary or until the trust assets are depleted.

Asset Protection

High — The assets in the trust are not considered the property of the beneficiary, providing strong protection from creditors and legal judgments.

Eligibility Requirements

The beneficiary must usually qualify for public assistance due to a disability as defined under the relevant government programs.

Favorable Jurisdictions

While SNTs are recognized in all states, jurisdictions like California, New York, and Florida have well-developed laws and community resources that support the effective use of these trusts.

Other Considerations

- The trust must be carefully structured to avoid direct cash distributions that could affect public assistance eligibility.

- Communication with family members about the trust's role and the importance of not disrupting public benefits is crucial.

Challenges & Limitations

- Managing the trust requires a deep understanding of benefit programs to avoid disqualifying the beneficiary.

- Can be emotionally challenging for families to balance the desire to provide directly with the need to maintain benefit eligibility.

Example

Parents of a child with autism could set-up a Special Needs Trust to ensure the kid has funds for therapies and care that are not covered by government programs. They set up the trust to fund these needs without affecting the child's Medicaid eligibility.

7. Life Insurance Trusts (ILITs)

Description

An ILIT, or Irrevocable Life Insurance Trust, specifically designed to manage and keep life insurance policies. This arrangement keeps the life insurance death benefit out of the grantor's taxable estate, thus bypassing estate taxes on the proceeds. By keeping the policy in an ILIT, beneficiaries can receive the death benefit free from both estate and income taxes, providing a clear financial benefit without additional tax burden.

Use Case(s)/When to Use

ILITs are used to provide liquidity and financial support to beneficiaries without increasing the taxable estate. They are especially beneficial in large estates where life insurance proceeds could significantly increase estate taxes. Additionally, they can supply funds for estate taxes, debts, or additional costs, eliminating the necessity to liquidate estate assets.

Who Should Be the Trustee

Typically, an independent or institutional trustee is chosen to manage the ILIT, as this helps maintain the necessary formalities to ensure the trust operates effectively and meets tax requirements.

Type

Irrevocable — Once established, the trust cannot be altered, and the grantor relinquishes authority over the life insurance policies moved into the trust.

Key Benefits

- Excludes the life insurance proceeds from the insured's estate, potentially saving significant amounts in estate taxes.
- Provides a tax-free benefit to beneficiaries, which could be utilized to settle estate taxes, debts, or other family duties.
- Protects the insurance proceeds from creditors and legal claims against the beneficiaries.

When It Is Created

Typically established during the grantor's lifetime to ensure that the life insurance policy is owned by the trust and not by the grantor at the time of death.

Tax Implications

The death proceeds obtained by the ILIT is exempt from estate and income taxes. Premiums paid into the trust are treated as gifts to the beneficiaries, using the annual gift tax exclusion if structured properly.

Control Over Assets

The trustee manages the policy within the trust, including the payment of premiums and the distribution of the death benefit according to the trust terms.

Duration

The ILIT exists until the life insurance policy proceeds are fully distributed according to the trust's terms, typically after the death of the insured.

Asset Protection

High — The proceeds are protected from the beneficiaries' creditors and any legal issues they might encounter.

Eligibility Requirements

The insured under the policy must be someone whose life the grantor has an insurable interest in. Beneficiaries must be specified but are not subject to other major restrictions.

Favorable Jurisdictions

Jurisdictions like South Dakota, Delaware, and Nevada are preferred for their favorable trust laws, which include privacy protections and advantageous tax treatment.

Other Considerations

- Proper structuring is crucial to avoid unintended tax consequences, especially regarding the transfer of existing policies into the trust.

- Regular reviews are needed to ensure that the ILIT is funded properly and that insurance policies remain in force.

Challenges & Limitations

- Once created, the grantor cannot alter the agreement or regain control over the life insurance policies.

- Incorrect setup or funding of the trust can lead to the proceeds being included in the estate, negating the tax benefits.

Example

A business owner with a $30 million estate sets up an ILIT and purchases a $10 million life insurance policy within the trust. This strategy ensures that the $10 million death benefit is not part of the estate, providing liquidity to pay estate taxes and support the family without additional estate tax burden.

8. Spendthrift Trusts

Description

Spendthrift Trusts aim to safeguard a beneficiary's inheritance from their own potential financial missteps, creditors, or complications arising from divorce. By restricting the beneficiary's access to the funds, the trust minimizes the risk that the beneficiary could squander their inheritance. The trustee has authority to make distributions according to the trust terms, often for the beneficiary's health, education, maintenance, and support.

Use Case(s)/When to Use

These trusts are ideal for beneficiaries who may not be financially responsible, who may be susceptible to external pressures that could result in poor financial decisions, or who have significant creditors. They ensure that the inheritance serves the beneficiary over time instead of being lost quickly.

Who Should Be the Trustee

An independent trustee, often a professional or institutional trustee, is usually appointed to provide impartial and structured management of the trust assets and to make distributions that are in the best interest of the beneficiary.

Type

Irrevocable — This ensures the trust provisions, especially the spendthrift clause, cannot be challenged or changed by the beneficiary.

Key Benefits

- Protects the trust's assets from the beneficiary's creditors, legal judgments, or other financial threats.

- Ensures that the beneficiary cannot directly access or squander the inheritance.

- Provides for the beneficiary's needs in a controlled and steady manner over time.

When It Is Created

Can be established at any time but is often created as part of a larger estate plan to provide long-term financial security for a beneficiary.

Tax Implications

Trust assets are typically subject to taxation at rates intended for trust income, which often exceed individual tax rates. Yet, meticulous planning can reduce the tax liability.

Control Over Assets

The trustee has full control over the timing and amount the beneficiary gets, within the guidelines set by the trust document.

Duration

The trust can last for a specified period, like until the recipient attains a specified age, or it can be designed to last for the beneficiary's lifetime.

Asset Protection

High — The beneficiary's creditors cannot access the trust assets, and the beneficiary's own actions are unlikely to jeopardize the inheritance.

Eligibility Requirements

There are no specific eligibility requirements for the beneficiary, other than those imposed by the grantor in the trust terms (e.g., age or milestone conditions).

Favorable Jurisdictions

States like Nevada, Delaware, and Alaska offer strong protections for spendthrift trusts, including enhanced privacy and creditor protection laws.

Other Considerations

- Regular assessments are necessary to ensure the distributions continue to meet the beneficiary's needs without enabling destructive behavior.

- The trust terms must be clear to prevent legal challenges from creditors or the beneficiary.

Challenges & Limitations

- Balancing distributions with the need to protect the beneficiary from their own decisions can be challenging.

- Potential conflicts can arise if the beneficiary disagrees with the trustee's management or distribution decisions.

Example

A parent sets up a spendthrift trust for a child who has shown a pattern of irresponsible spending and debt accumulation. The trust provides the child with a monthly allowance and pays for essentials like housing and medical care, ensuring the child is supported without risking the principal.

9. Totten Trusts (Payable on Death Accounts)

Description

Totten Trusts, also known as Payable-on-death (POD) accounts, are a straightforward and informal trust arrangement where a bank account is designated to pass directly to a named beneficiary upon the account holder's death. This setup bypasses the probate process and allows for the swift transfer of the account's balance to the beneficiary, ensuring they have access to the funds avoiding the delays and expenses linked to the probate process.

Use Case(s)/When to Use

These trusts are used for their simplicity and ease of setup, often to ensure that a specific beneficiary has immediate access to cash to pay for immediate expenses following the grantor's death. They are ideal for smaller estates or when the grantor wishes to provide a beneficiary with a non-probate asset quickly and without complication.

Who Should Be the Trustee

There is no trustee in the traditional sense because these are essentially beneficiary designations on a bank account. The account holder maintains full control over the account while they are alive.

Type

Revocable — The account holder can change the beneficiary or close the account at any time before their death.

Key Benefits

- Simple and cost-effective way to transfer assets outside of probate.

- Immediate access to funds for the beneficiary upon the account holder's death.

- Minimizes the legal and administrative burdens typically associated with transferring assets through a will.

When It Is Created

During the account holder's lifetime by filling out a designated beneficiary form with the bank or financial institution.

Tax Implications

There are no immediate tax implications for setting up a Totten Trust, but the funds may incur inheritance or estate taxes based on the jurisdiction and entire magnitude of the estate.

Control Over Assets

The account holder retains complete control over the funds until their death, at which point the named beneficiary gains immediate access to the remaining balance.

Duration

Lasts until the passing of the account owner, after which the money are transferred straight to the beneficiary.

Asset Protection

Moderate — While the funds are protected from probate, they may be considered in the account holder's estate for debt repayment before being distributed to the beneficiary.

Eligibility Requirements

The beneficiary must be clearly named, but there are no other specific requirements. The arrangement is recognized by most financial institutions.

Favorable Jurisdictions

Totten Trusts are recognized in all U.S. states, but the specifics can vary slightly by state. Generally, the simplicity of these trusts makes them widely accessible and utilized.

Other Considerations

- The account should be monitored to ensure that it aligns with the overall estate plan and that beneficiary designations are up to date to ensure the desired outcome upon the account holder's death.

Challenges & Limitations

- These trusts cannot hold assets other than the funds in the specific account.

- While straightforward, they lack the flexibility and protection offered by more complex trust structures, especially against legal challenges or creditors.

Example

A grandmother sets up a Totten Trust by designating her grandson as the beneficiary on her savings account. Upon her death, the grandson immediately accesses the funds to cover funeral expenses and other costs without waiting for probate or other estate settlement processes.

10. Dynasty Trusts

Description

A Dynasty Trust is structured to endure across several generations, possibly indefinitely, based on state laws. These trusts are structured to pass wealth down to the grantor's descendants while avoiding the transfer taxes that typically apply to each generation's inheritance. By putting assets in a Dynasty Trust, families can preserve wealth for an extended period, protecting it from estate taxes, creditors, divorces, and other risks that could erode family assets over time.

Use Case(s)/When to Use

These trusts are utilized by families looking to maintain and grow wealth across several generations without the repeated application of estate and gift taxes with each transfer. They are perfect for affluent individuals aiming to safeguard their wealth for several forthcoming generations of their family.

Who Should Be the Trustee

Considering the extended duration of these trusts, a professional or institutional trustee is often necessary to manage the trust's assets and distribution strategy effectively over decades or even centuries.

Type

Irrevocable — To maintain the trust's tax benefits and protective features, it is set up as irrevocable from the outset.

Key Benefits

- Preserves wealth across multiple generations, minimizing estate and gift taxes for each transfer.
- Protects assets from beneficiaries' creditors, divorces, and potential lawsuits.
- Provides a structured framework for family wealth management and succession.

When It Is Created

Usually established during the grantor's life to maximize the benefits of tax optimization and protection of wealth.

Tax Implications

Significantly reduces or eliminates estate taxes over multiple generations due to the exemption from generation-skipping transfer taxes (GSTT) up to a certain limit and careful planning around exemptions.

Control Over Assets

The trustee manages the trust assets according to the trust agreement, with beneficiaries generally having limited direct control, which helps preserve assets in line with the grantor's vision.

Duration

Can last for multiple generations, often up to 21 years after the death of the last beneficiary alive at the trust's creation, or even longer in states that have repealed the Rule Against Perpetuities.

Asset Protection

Very high — The trust structure provides robust protection from creditors and legal claims, ensuring that assets remain within the family as intended by the grantor.

Eligibility Requirements

No specific eligibility requirements for beneficiaries other than being descendants or family members specified by the grantor. Trusts must be structured to comply with applicable state laws to achieve the desired duration and tax benefits.

Favorable Jurisdictions

States like South Dakota, Delaware, Alaska, and Nevada are particularly favorable for Dynasty Trusts due to their favorable trust laws, including extended perpetuity periods and strong asset protection statutes.

Other Considerations

- These trusts require careful legal and financial planning to navigate and adhere to intricate tax laws and trust protocols.

- Families should consider the impact of long-term asset management and potential changes in family circumstances over generations.

Challenges & Limitations

- Complexity in setup and maintenance can be high, requiring ongoing legal and financial expertise.

- Potential challenges in adapting the trust's terms to future changes in laws, family structure, or asset characteristics.

Example

A family establishes a Dynasty Trust with $50 million in assets, aiming to provide for education, health, and maintenance of their descendants. The trust is structured to distribute income and principal under specific conditions while protecting the assets from estate taxes and creditors for potentially 100 years or more, depending on state law.

11. Charitable Trusts

Description

Charitable Trusts are created to help charitable organizations, offering tax advantages while also potentially providing income to individuals who are not involved in charitable activities. There are two main types of charitable trusts. In one, called a Charitable Lead Trust (CLT), a charity receives income for a specified duration, following that the residual assets are moved to non-charitable beneficiaries. The other type, known as a Charitable Remainder Trust (CRT), works in reverse: non-charitable heirs receive income initially, with the charity receiving the remaining assets afterward.

Use Case(s)/When to Use

These trusts are used when individuals wish to back philanthropic efforts while also obtaining tax advantages and maintaining some benefit for themselves or other non-charitable beneficiaries. CLTs are ideal for those who want to give to charity now and leave the remainder to heirs, while CRTs are suited for those looking to receive income during their lifetime and benefit a charity afterward.

Who Should Be the Trustee

Typically managed by an independent trustee or financial institution, especially when complex assets or multiple charities are involved, to ensure the trust complies with all legal requirements and its charitable goals are met.

Type

Irrevocable — This is necessary to qualify for the tax benefits associated with charitable giving.

Key Benefits

- Provides significant tax benefits, including income, gift, and estate tax reductions.
- Supports charitable causes in a structured way, potentially over a long period.
- Can provide a steady income stream to non-charitable beneficiaries in the case of CRTs.

When It Is Created

Can be established during the grantor's lifetime for immediate tax benefits or as part of a testamentary strategy to implement after the grantor's death.

Tax Implications

Provides instant income tax deductions for the value of the charitable interest in the trust. Estate tax implications can be favorable, particularly if the trust is structured to extract assets from the grantor's taxable estate.

Control Over Assets

The trustee manages the assets and the distributions, balancing the needs of both charitable and non-charitable beneficiaries according to the trust terms.

Duration

CLTs continue for a determined period or for the duration of the grantor's life, while CRTs typically last for the lifetimes of the non-charitable beneficiaries or a term of up to 20 years.

Asset Protection

Moderate — While the charitable portion of the trust is protected from creditors, the income streams to non-charitable beneficiaries may be accessible to their creditors, depending on the structure.

Eligibility Requirements

The charitable beneficiary must be a qualified charitable organization. Non-charitable beneficiaries are typically specified by the grantor and can be anyone the grantor chooses.

Favorable Jurisdictions

Jurisdictions with favorable trust laws, such as Delaware, South Dakota, and Nevada, are often chosen for these trusts due to their tax advantages and flexible structures.

Other Considerations

- Structuring these trusts requires a careful balance between charitable giving and maintaining sufficient benefits for non-charitable beneficiaries.

- Regular monitoring and adjustments may be necessary to respond to changes in tax laws or personal circumstances.

Challenges & Limitations

- Balancing the interests of charitable and non-charitable beneficiaries can be complex.

- Requires careful planning to ensure the trust meets all IRS requirements for charitable trusts to maintain its tax benefits.

Example

An individual sets up a CRT, transferring $1 million into the trust. The CRT provides the individual with an ongoing yearly return of 4% of the trust's value for their lifetime, followed by the donation of any remaining assets to a designated charity, ensuring the individual benefits during their lifetime and the charity receives support afterward.

12. Qualified Personal Residence Trust (QPRT)

Description

A Qualified Personal Residence Trust (QPRT) enables someone to place their own home or vacation property into a trust. They can still live there for a set number of years after transferring ownership. After this period, the ownership is passed to beneficiaries, typically the grantor's children, with reduced gift tax costs, as the gift is valued at the present considering the interest (the person will continue to live there) in thé home, not its full value at the time of the transfer.

Use Case(s)/When to Use

QPRTs are particularly useful for individuals who want to pass their home to their heirs while minimizing the taxable portion of their estate. They allow the grantor to continue living in the home while freezing its value for estate tax considerations when the trust is established.

Who Should Be the Trustee

An independent trustee is often recommended to ensure the trust complies with all legal requirements, but the grantor can also serve as trustee in some cases.

Type

Irrevocable — Once established, the QPRT terms cannot be changed, and the home's future ownership is set.

Key Benefits

- Reduces the gift tax value of the home when transferred to beneficiaries.

- Allows the grantor to keep staying in the property for the term specified.

- Freezes the home's valuation for estate tax considerations when the trust is established, potentially saving significant estate taxes.

When It Is Created

During the grantor's lifetime, to maximize the benefits of transferring the home out of their estate.

Tax Implications

The initial transferring to the QPRT is viewed as gifting the remainder interest, utilizing a portion of the lifetime gift tax exclusion for the grantor based on the home's current value. The grantor must outlive the QPRT term for the tax benefits to be fully realized.

Control Over Assets

The grantor can reside in the home during the QPRT term but loses control afterward unless they pay rent.

Duration

The trust lasts for a specified term chosen by the grantor (typically between 10-15 years). This duration is critical because the grantor must outlive this term for the estate tax benefits to be realized. If the grantor passes away during this term, the full value of the home is included in their estate for tax purposes.

Asset Protection

Moderate — During the QPRT term, the home is somewhat protected from the grantor's creditors, but this protection is stronger after the home passes to the beneficiaries.

Eligibility Requirements

The grantor must own the home and must outlive the QPRT term for the strategy to be effective in reducing estate taxes.

Favorable Jurisdictions

While QPRTs are recognized under federal tax law across all states, jurisdictions like Florida and California are often chosen for their favorable real estate and trust laws, particularly regarding homestead exemptions and property tax implications.

Other Considerations

- The grantor can rent the home from the trust after the QPRT term to continue living there, which can provide additional income to the trust.

- Accurate valuation of the property when it is transferred and careful planning of the term are essential to maximize benefits.

Challenges & Limitations

- If the grantor dies before the QPRT term ends, the tax advantages are forfeited, and the property becomes part of the estate.

- Managing the trust and property can involve ongoing expenses, including maintenance and property taxes, which need careful planning.

Example

A person moves their $2 million home into a QPRT with a 15-year period. The discounted value of the remainder interest is $1 million. This means the taxable gift is $1 million instead of $2 million. If the individual survives the 15-year period, the home is passed to their children, avoiding inclusion in their estate.

13. Grantor Retained Interest Trusts (GRITs)

Description

A Grantor Retained Interest Trust (GRIT) is a special kind of trust where the person creating it transfers assets into the trust but continues to earn income from those assets for a designated time. Following this interval, the residual assets are transferred to the beneficiaries. This structure allows the grantor to reduce the gift's value for tax purposes due to their retained interest, thus lowering potential gift taxes on the transfer.

Use Case(s)/When to Use

GRITs are particularly effective for transferring appreciating assets to beneficiaries at a reduced tax cost while the grantor retains some benefits, like income, for a period. They are used when assets are anticipated to increase considerably in value, facilitating the transfer of future growth to the receivers without additional taxes.

Who Should Be the Trustee

An independent or institutional trustee is frequently selected to guarantee the trust is administered as specified and to uphold its tax integrity.

Type

Irrevocable — Ensures that the assets transferred into the trust are permanently removed from the grantor's estate for estate tax purposes.

Key Benefits

- Reduces the taxable gift amount by allowing the grantor to retain an income interest.

- Allows significant assets to be transferred to beneficiaries at a reduced tax cost.

- Can be an effective tool to transfer wealth without using as much of the grantor's gift and estate tax exemption.

When It Is Created

Typically established during the grantor's lifetime to facilitate the transfer of assets and the realization of tax benefits.

Tax Implications

The initial gift's value is diminished by the grantor's reserved interest, determined using IRS tables and the duration of the income interest. This leads to lower gift taxes compared to transferring the assets outright.

Control Over Assets

The grantor retains the right to income from the trust for the specified term but does not control the ultimate disposition of the trust assets, which is determined by the trust terms.

Duration

Set for a specific term based on the grantor's planning objectives, often several years. After this term, whatever is left of the assets goes to the beneficiaries.

Asset Protection

Moderate — The trust provides some protection from creditors for the assets, particularly after the grantor's retained interest term ends.

Eligibility Requirements

There are no specific eligibility requirements for the beneficiaries. The trust must be structured correctly to ensure that the grantor's retained interest is recognized for tax purposes.

Favorable Jurisdictions

States with favorable trust laws, like South Dakota, Delaware, and Alaska, are often chosen for GRITs due to their flexibility and the asset protection they offer.

Other Considerations

- Careful structuring is required to ensure that the GRIT achieves the intended tax benefits without unintended consequences.

- Regular reviews and valuations are needed to ensure that the GRIT continues to meet its objectives, especially if asset values change significantly.

Challenges & Limitations

- The grantor must survive the term of the trust for the tax benefits to be fully realized.

- Overseeing the trust and ensuring the respect of IRS rules can be complex and require specialized advice.

Example

An artist transfers a collection of art valued at $5 million into a GRIT with a 10-year term, retaining the right to any income generated. The present value of the gift is $3 million due to the reserved interest. If the artist survives the term, the appreciated value of the art (say $7 million) passes to the kids with no additional gift tax.

14. Grantor Retained Annuity Trusts (GRATs)

Description

Grantor Retained Annuity Trusts (GRATs) are a financial tool used to move asset appreciation to recipients without significant gift taxes. The grantor places assets into the GRAT and retains the right to receive an annual annuity payment for a fixed term. At the term's conclusion, any remaining assets transfer to the beneficiaries. The key is that the value of the gift is reduced by the grantor's annuity interest, minimizing the gift tax implications.

Use Case(s)/When to Use

GRATs are particularly effective for transferring high-growth assets like stock in a family business or shares in a fast-growing company. They enable the grantor to lock in the value of the transferred assets at the trust's inception, allowing any increase in value to pass to beneficiaries without incurring extra taxes.

Who Should Be the Trustee

An independent trustee is recommended to manage the GRAT and ensure that annuity payments are made correctly and that the GRAT's terms are followed to comply with IRS regulations.

Type

Irrevocable — The structure and terms are fixed once the GRAT is established, which is necessary to secure the intended tax advantages.

Key Benefits

- Allows the grantor to pass on asset growth to beneficiaries at minimal gift tax cost.

- Delivers a consistent income flow to the grantor during the GRAT term, which can be useful for retirement planning or other needs.

- Effective in estate planning to reduce the taxable estate without using a significant portion of the grantor's lifetime exemption.

When It Is Created

During the grantor's lifetime, to allow the transfer of appreciating assets and the realization of the strategy's tax benefits.

Tax Implications

The initial gift's valorization is reduced by the present value of the annuity payments the grantor retains, considering the IRS interest rates when the GRAT's is formed. Any growth exceeding these rates transfers to the beneficiaries without incurring extra taxes.

Control Over Assets

The grantor receives annuity payments but does not control the remainder interest, which is what passes to the beneficiaries after the GRAT term.

Duration

Typically set for a relatively short term, such as 2-10 years, based on the grantor's objectives and the anticipated growth of the assets.

Asset Protection

Moderate — The assets are somewhat protected from the grantor's creditors during the GRAT term, especially the remainder interest.

Eligibility Requirements

No specific eligibility requirements for the beneficiaries, but the structure must meet IRS guidelines to ensure the GRAT's tax benefits are realized.

Favorable Jurisdictions

States like Nevada, South Dakota, and Delaware, known for their favorable trust environments, are often preferred for establishing GRATs due to their legal support for such structures and potential state tax advantages.

Other Considerations

- The GRAT's success heavily depends on the assets' performance exceeding the IRS's assumed interest rates; careful selection of assets is crucial.

- The grantor must survive the GRAT term for the benefits to be fully realized, making the choice of term length a critical decision.

Challenges & Limitations

- If the person who established the trust (grantor) passes away before the end of the GRAT term, the tax advantages might not apply anymore, and the assets could become part of the grantor's estate.

- The GRAT's fixed annuity payments mean that the grantor cannot adjust them in response to changes in their financial needs or asset performance.

Example

A tech entrepreneur places $10 million of startup shares into a 5-year GRAT when the shares are expected to appreciate significantly. They receive an annual annuity based on the initial value, and at the end of the term, the appreciated shares (now worth $20 million) pass to their children with no additional gift tax on the appreciation.

15. Grantor Retained Unitrusts (GRUTs)

Description

Grantor Retained Unitrusts (GRUTs) involve the grantor moving assets into a trust while retaining the right to an annual payment, which is a fixed percentage of the trust's value, recalculated annually. This setup enables the grantor to gain from heightened income if the trust assets appreciate in value over time. When the trust period concludes, the residual assets are passed on to the beneficiaries. This structure is particularly beneficial for assets expected to grow in value because it provides a hedge against inflation and increases the grantor's income potential over the trust term.

Use Case(s)/When to Use

GRUTs are particularly useful for grantors who expect the trust assets to appreciate and wish to receive a variable pay out of the entire value of those assets. They are ideal for grantors looking to pass on appreciating assets to beneficiaries while maintaining a revenue flow that could increase if the assets perform well.

Who Should Be the Trustee

An independent trustee or a professional financial institution is recommended to manage the GRUT's assets and confirm that annual disbursements are recalculated and correctly paid in accordance with the trust terms.

Type

Irrevocable — This ensures that the GRUT provides the planned tax and estate planning benefits by removing the transferred assets from the grantor's estate.

Key Benefits

- Provides the grantor with an income stream that can increase if the trust assets appreciate, offering potential hedge against inflation.

- Allows for significant estate and gift tax planning opportunities, as the value of the gift to beneficiaries is reduced by the present value of the grantor's retained unitrust interest.

- Enables the transfer of asset appreciation to beneficiaries without additional taxation.

When It Is Created

Usually established during the grantor's lifetime to facilitate the immediate transfer of assets and begin the period of retained income.

Tax Implications

The initial transfer to the GRUT is a taxable gift, but its value is discounted by the value of the retained interest, based on IRS valuation tables and the expected duration of the trust. This leads to potential savings on gift taxes. The grantor is taxed on the income distributed each year.

Control Over Assets

The trustee manages the trust assets, but the grantor receives a variable annual payment based on a fixed percentage of the trust's assets, recalculated annually.

Duration

Typically established for a specified term of years or for the life of the grantor. After this term, the remaining trust assets pass to the beneficiaries.

Asset Protection

Moderate — The trust provides protection against creditors for the beneficiaries' remainder interest and offers the grantor some income stability with potential growth.

Eligibility Requirements

There are no specific eligibility requirements for the beneficiaries, but the trust must be structured properly to ensure the unitrust payments and eventual transfer to beneficiaries achieve the desired tax benefits.

Favorable Jurisdictions

States like Delaware, South Dakota, and Nevada offer legal environments that support the effective use of GRUTs due to their favorable trust laws and privacy protections.

Other Considerations

- The annual revaluation means the income can vary significantly, requiring the grantor to be prepared for fluctuating income levels.

- Asset selection is crucial as the performance of the trust assets directly impacts the grantor's annual income.

Challenges & Limitations

- The variable income can be a risk if the trust assets decrease in value, potentially decreasing the grantor's annual income.

- Complex valuation and annual recalculations require meticulous management and accurate appraisals.

Example

A grantor transfers a vacation property valued at $1 million into a GRUT, retaining the right to an annual payment of 5% of the trust's assets, recalculated annually. If the property appreciates to $1.5 million over a few years, the annual payment increases, providing the grantor with a higher income. At the end of the period, the asset passes to the beneficiaries, potentially with significant tax savings on the appreciation.

|Part 4| Considerations for Business Owners

Section 20: Estate Planning for Business Owners

Understanding the Context

As a business owner, your estate planning needs are unique. You're not just planning for the distribution of your personal assets; you're also considering the future of your business. The decisions you make now will affect not just your financial security but also the livelihood of your employees and the legacy you leave behind. This process involves much more than drafting a will—it requires a comprehensive strategy to ensure both your personal assets and business interests are protected and passed on according to your vision.

Estate planning for you involves a delicate balance between personal and business interests. You need to navigate through complex legal, tax, and financial landscapes to create a plan that follows your objectives and supports the people and causes you care about. If you're seeking to facilitate a seamless handover of your business to the future generation, protect your assets from creditors, or minimize the burden of estate taxes, a well-crafted estate plan is essential.

The future is unpredictable, but with proper estate planning, you can prepare for various scenarios and ensure that your business doesn't just survive but thrives, even in your absence. Think about what happens if you suddenly aren't there to make decisions: Who will take over the business? How will your assets be distributed? Will your family be financially secure? These are questions that need answers, and those answers should be spelled out in your estate plan. Your main goals in estate planning likely include:

- Ensuring Business Continuity: You want your business to continue operating smoothly without you, which means planning for who will take over and how they will run the business.

- Protecting Your Assets: You need strategies to safeguard both your personal and business assets from potential threats like lawsuits, creditors, and excessive taxation.

- Caring for Your Loved Ones: It's about making sure that your family is provided for in the way you intend, especially if they are not involved in the business.

- Minimizing Taxes: Efficient tax planning can substantially lower the estate taxes your heirs may face, preserving more of your estate for them to enjoy.

- Leaving a Legacy: Beyond money and assets, it's about the mark you leave on the world, including charitable giving and ensuring your business upholds your values.

Succession Planning

Succession planning is more than just a strategy; it's a critical part of securing the future of your business and ensuring that your legacy endures. As you think about the future, you face the question of who will take over your business when you're no longer able to lead. This process involves identifying potential leaders and preparing them to take over at the right time, ensuring a seamless transition that maintains the stability and continuity of your business.

For you, succession planning is about preparing for the future by guaranteeing that your business has the necessary leadership to maintain operations effectively, even without you. It's about making sure that the vision and values you've instilled in your company persist through the next generation of leadership.

Preparing for Succession

1. Identifying Potential Successors: Start by looking within your family and your company for individuals who demonstrate the skills and desire to take over the business. Consider their experience, commitment to the business, and ability to lead. If no suitable internal candidates are available, you might look externally. The key is to identify individuals who not only have the skills but also share your vision for the business.

2. Training and Developing Successors: Once you've identified potential successors, the next step is to prepare them for future leadership roles. This involves training them in all aspects of the business, from day-to-day operations to strategic planning. Mentorship programs, leadership training, and hands-on experience in various roles can all play a part in equipping your chosen successor with the knowledge and skills they need to lead the business successfully.

3. Setting Up a Transition Plan: A clear transition plan specifies the timing and process for leadership transfer and ownership. It should include timelines, training goals, and any milestones that successors need to achieve before they can take over. This plan not only guides the development of potential successors but also helps the entire business prepare for the change in leadership.

Managing Family Dynamics and Business Needs

If your business is family-owned, succession planning can be particularly complex. Navigating family relationships alongside business demands necessitates a meticulous strategy:

- Communication is Key: Open and honest communication with family members about the future of the business is crucial. Talking about everyone's roles, what we expect from each other, and where we see the business heading can really help us avoid misunderstandings and conflicts.

- Fairness Over Equality: In family businesses, it's often more practical to think in terms of fairness rather than equality. Not all family members will have an equal interest or role in the business, and the succession plan should mirror the contributions and interests of each participant.

- External Advisors: Bringing in external advisors such as estate planners, business attorneys, and financial advisors offer unbiased guidance and assist in navigating the complex issues that can arise in family-owned businesses.

Legal and Financial Considerations

- Legal Agreements: Ensure all legal aspects of the succession are addressed, including updating wills, trusts, and buy-sell agreements to reflect the succession plan.

- Valuation of the Business: Accurately valuing the business is crucial for a fair transfer of ownership. Use professional appraisers to get an accurate estimate of the business's worth.

- Tax Planning: Work in collaboration with tax experts to reduce the tax consequences of transferring ownership. One effective approach is gradually transferring ownership shares of the business to family members, which can help lower taxes in the long run.

Asset Protection

Asset protection strategies aim to build legal and financial defenses that shield both your business and personal assets from various risks, such as lawsuits, creditors, and financial downturns. By implementing these strategies, you guarantee that your diligently accumulated assets are maintained for your beneficiaries and that your business can weather unexpected challenges.

As a business owner, you're exposed to various risks that could threaten your personal and business assets. These might include legal claims from customers, suppliers, or employees; financial liabilities from loans or other obligations; and even issues related to divorce or personal creditors. Protecting your assets ensures that these risks don't jeopardize your financial security or the operational stability of your business.

Strategies to Safeguard Your Assets

Utilizing the Right Business Structure

One of the first lines of defense in asset protection is choosing the appropriate structure for your business. Various business structures provide distinct levels of shielding:

- Limited Liability Companies (LLCs): LLCs provide a shield for your personal possessions from your business liabilities. The implication is that creditors can usually only pursue the assets within the LLC and not your personal assets.

- Corporations (S-Corps, C-Corps): Similar to LLCs, corporations offer limited liability protection. Your personal assets are generally protected from business debts and legal judgments against the corporation.

- Partnerships (Limited Partnerships, Limited Liability Partnerships): These structures can offer some protection for partners, with limited liability partners protected from the debts and liabilities of the partnership.

Leveraging Trusts for Asset Protection

Trusts can serve as an effective means to safeguard your assets:

- Irrevocable Trusts: Once assets are placed in an irrevocable trust, ownership transfers from the original owner; the trust becomes their legal owner. This separation from your estate means these assets are typically beyond the reach of personal creditors and legal actions.

- Domestic Asset Protection Trusts (DAPT): Accessible in few states, these trusts let you to shield assets from creditors while still benefiting from the assets under certain conditions.

Equity Stripping

Equity stripping is a strategy to reduce the attractiveness of your assets to creditors by diminishing the equity available in them:

- Liens and Loans: By placing liens on property or taking out loans secured by your assets, you reduce the actual equity in these assets, making them less appealing to creditors.

Retirement Plans and Asset Protection

Certain retirement plans are favored under federal law for asset protection:

- Qualified Retirement Plans (401(k)s, IRAs): These plans often have substantial protection under federal law from creditors. For example, ERISA-qualified retirement plans offer almost unlimited protection from creditors under federal law.

Insurance as a Layer of Protection

Insurance is an essential strategy in protecting your assets:

- Professional Liability Insurance: This can protect your business from claims related to errors, malpractice, or negligence.

- Umbrella Insurance: This extends coverage beyond your standard policy limits, providing an additional layer of security.

- Homestead Protection: Some states have homestead laws that protect a portion of your home's value from creditors.

Key Benefits of Asset Protection Strategies

- Peace of Mind: Being aware that your assets are secure allows you to concentrate more on growing your business and less on what could go wrong.

- Financial Security for Heirs: Ensures that your estate passes to your beneficiaries without being depleted by creditors or lawsuits.

- Business Continuity: Protects your business assets, helping ensure that your business can continue to operate through challenging times.

Best Practices in Implementing Asset Protection

- Early Implementation: The optimal time to establish asset protection strategies is before any risks emerge. Proactive planning can be more effective and easier to defend legally.

- Compliance and Legality: Ensure that all asset protection strategies comply with legal standards to avoid issues of fraudulence or evasion.

- Professional Advice: Collaborate with legal and financial experts who focus on asset protection to tailor tactics to your exact needs and to stay abreast of changes in laws and regulations.

Buy-Sell Agreements

When you're considering how to ensure that your business transitions smoothly should you pass away, become incapacitated, or retire, one of the principal elements you should study is a buy-sell agreement. This agreement is a critical tool that keeps your business steady and under the control of those you trust, while also providing for your family's financial security.

A buy-sell agreement essentially lays out how your interest in the business will be reallocated if you can no longer run the business due to death, disability, or other circumstances. Think of it as a sort of business will. It helps prevent potential conflict among remaining owners and your family and ensures that everyone knows what will happen and how it will happen.

The core idea of a buy-sell agreement is that it locks in a plan for the future of your business shares or ownership interests. This agreement can be set up in several ways on the base of the organization of your business and your specific needs.

Types of Buy-Sell Agreements

1. Cross-Purchase Agreements: In this type, if something happens to you, your co-owners can buy your share at a predetermined price. This method is often preferred because it provides a clear and straightforward path for the remaining owners to keep the business in their control.

2. Redemption Agreements: Here, the business itself is set up to buy back your share. This can be simpler in terms of fewer transactions and might be easier to manage administratively.

3. Hybrid Agreements: As the name suggests, these agreements combine elements of both cross-purchase and redemption agreements. They provide flexibility, allowing the remaining owners and the business itself to decide the best course of action when the time comes.

Funding Buy-Sell Agreements with Life Insurance

One of the most common and efficient method to finance a buy-sell agreement is by using life insurance. Here's how it typically works:

- Life Insurance Policies: You, or the business, take out life insurance policies on the lives of each partner in the business. The reason for this is simple – life insurance can provide the necessary funds to buy out your share if you pass away unexpectedly.

- Immediate Liquidity: When you die, the life insurance policy disburses a death benefit to the policyholder, which is then used to buy your share of the business from your estate. This means that your family gets a fair price for your ownership of the business, and the business carries on operating with no need to liquidate other assets to pay for the buyout.

Why Is This Important for You?

- Security for Your Family: With a funded buy-sell agreement, you have the reassurance that your family will be compensated fairly and promptly for your business interest. Your family won't have to worry about negotiating with your co-owners or dealing with the business directly during a difficult time.

- Stability for Your Business: For your business, a buy-sell agreement funded by life insurance means that the transition of your share can happen smoothly without financial strain. The business doesn't have to come up with a large sum of money on short notice, which can be especially important if your death or incapacitation happens during a challenging economic period.

- Clarity and Fairness: These agreements provide a clear and agreed-upon path for the transition of your business interest, which can prevent disputes among your family and co-owners. It sets expectations and provides a structured plan that everyone has agreed to ahead of time.

The Process of Setting Up a Buy-Sell Agreement

To set up a buy-sell agreement, you'll want to start by consulting with your business partners, a financial advisor, and a legal professional. Here's a simplified path you might follow:

1. Discussion and Agreement: Talk with your business partners about the need for a buy-sell agreement. Discuss how each of you wants the business to proceed in the event of someone's departure or death.

2. Choose the Right Type of Agreement: Decide if a cross-purchase, redemption, or hybrid agreement is best for your situation based on the specificities and size of your business.

3. Determine the Valuation Method: Agree on how your business should be valued for the purposes of the buy-sell agreement. That could mean also using the services of a valuation expert or agreeing on a formula or method that can be applied.

4. Work with Professionals: Have a lawyer draft the agreement to ensure that all legal aspects are covered. Then, work with a financial advisor to arrange the funding, often through life insurance, to ensure that money will be available to execute the agreement when needed.

5. Review Regularly: Over time, your business will grow and change, and so might your personal situation. Regularly revising and updating your buy-sell agreement is essential to keep it relevant and that continues to work effectively for your needs.

Section 21: Understanding and Managing Digital Assets in Your Estate Planning

In today's digital age, your estate planning needs to encompass not just physical and financial assets but also digital assets. These are parts of your digital life and identity that hold both sentimental and monetary value. Recognizing and planning for these assets can prevent potential complications and ensure they are handled according to your wishes.

Digital assets encompass all content or electronic data that you possess and are authorized to utilize. These resources are available digitally and can be easily recognized. What makes them particularly valuable is that they often come with rights to use, sell, publish, or distribute.

What Digital Assets Are

1. Online Financial Accounts: This includes everything from your online banking and brokerage accounts to digital wallets like PayPal or Venmo.

2. Social Media Accounts: Platforms like Facebook, Twitter, Instagram, and LinkedIn, where you interact with others and share parts of your life.

3. Email Accounts: Your personal and business email accounts are crucial as they often serve as a hub for communication and store important information and contacts.

4. Digital Photos and Videos: Memories stored digitally on your devices or in the cloud, capturing moments you cherish.

5. Digital Business Assets: This could include your business's online presence, such as websites, blogs, and e-commerce platforms, as well as digital products or services you offer.

6. Online Subscriptions and Loyalty Programs: Memberships or recurring subscriptions, as well as points accumulated in loyalty programs.

7. Cryptocurrency: Digital currencies like Bitcoin, Ethereum, or any of the myriad other cryptocurrencies represent significant digital assets.

8. Intellectual Property: Digital files for patents, trademarks, copyrighted materials, software code, and designs.

What Digital Assets Are Not

1. Physical Devices: While your smartphone, computer, or tablet may be necessary to access your digital assets, the devices themselves are considered personal property, not digital assets.

2. Software That Is Not Owned: If you use software or databases under a license that does not grant ownership, these are not your digital assets; you're simply allowed to use them.

3. Services Without Transferable Value: Online services where you participate but do not have an account or any ownership, like reading articles on a news website, don't count as digital assets.

Why Including Digital Assets in Your Estate Planning Is Important

Your digital assets, from your email accounts to your social media profiles and digital currencies, play a significant role in your personal and business life. Including these assets in your estate planning ensures that:

- Access to Important Information: Your executors and heirs can access critical information that may be necessary for settling your estate.

- Financial Value Is Retained: Assets like domain names or cryptocurrency can have significant monetary value that should be considered and protected.

- Sentimental Memories Are Preserved: Digital photos and videos often hold irreplaceable memories. Ensuring these are passed on can mean a lot to your loved ones.

- Continuity for Online Businesses: If you run an online business, proper planning ensures that your business can continue without disruption.

- Privacy and Security: Proper planning includes handling your digital assets in ways that maintain your privacy and security, even after your death.

How to Include Digital Assets in Your Estate Planning

To properly incorporate your digital assets into your estate planning, here are practical steps you can take:

1. Make an Inventory: Start by listing all your digital assets. This list should include login URLs, usernames, passwords, and any other necessary information to access each asset. Consider using a password manager or another secure tool to store this information safely yet conveniently accessible.

2. Update Your Will and Power of Attorney: Clearly state in your will how you want your digital assets to be handled. Make sure to revise your power of attorney so that your chosen representative can handle your online accounts and digital assets in case you're unable to.

3. Provide Access Instructions: Make sure your executor and anyone else you designate to handle your digital assets know how to access the inventory you've created. This might involve using a digital executor—a person specifically designated to manage your digital assets.

4. Outline Your Wishes: For each digital asset, specify what you want to happen to it. For example, you might want your social media profiles to be turned into memorial accounts or deleted entirely. For business-related digital assets, you may need to provide instructions for transferring ownership or managing the asset for continuity.

5. Consider Legal Requirements: Some digital assets, especially those involving copyright or other intellectual property, may have specific legal requirements for transfer or management. Work with an attorney to ensure your plans comply with existing laws.

Who to Designate to Manage Your Digital Assets

Selecting the ideal individual to oversee your digital assets is just as vital as the initial planning. This person, often called a digital executor, should be someone who is:

- Technologically Savvy: Able to navigate various digital platforms and understand the basics of digital security.

- Trustworthy: Handling sensitive information with the discretion and respect it deserves.

- Legally Empowered: Has the legal authority, as specified in your will or estate plan, to act on your behalf in managing these assets.

You might choose one person to handle both your digital and physical assets, or you might find it better to have one executor for each, especially if your digital assets are extensive or complicated.

Complications from Not Managing Digital Assets

Failing to manage and plan for your digital assets can lead to several complications:

- Loss of Assets: Without your passwords and access instructions, valuable assets like cryptocurrency or online accounts could be lost forever.

- Identity Theft: If your digital assets are not properly secured or managed, they could attract identity thieves, adding more complexity to your estate.

- Emotional Distress for Family Members: Imagine the added stress on your loved ones if they cannot access photos, videos, or other sentimental digital assets because there was no plan in place.

- Disruption of Online Businesses: If you run an online business, failing to plan can lead to operational disruptions that could have financial implications for your heirs.

By including digital assets in your estate plan, you not only protect these valuable and sentimental assets but also provide clear guidance to those you leave behind, ensuring that your digital legacy is handled exactly as you wish.

|Part 5| Optimization Strategies

Section 22: Tax Optimization

Leveraging the Lifetime Gift Tax Exemption

The Lifetime Gift Tax Exemption plays a crucial role in thoughtful estate planning, enabling individuals to pass on significant assets without worrying about federal gift and estate taxes during their lifetime.

The Lifetime Gift Tax Exemption, as part of US federal tax law, permits individuals to give away a specific amount of assets over their lifetime without incurring taxes, separate from the yearly gift tax exclusion. As of 2024, this exemption amount is $13.61 mln per individual. This allows a person to gift up to this sum throughout their lifetime without facing federal gift tax.

Benefits of Using the Lifetime Gift Tax Exemption

1. Tax Reduction: By transferring assets within the exemption limits, individuals can significantly reduce or eliminate federal gift taxes that might otherwise be levied on large transfers.

2. Estate Size Management: Using this exemption can greatly reduce the estate's taxable value, which may reduce or even eliminate the federal estate taxes their heirs must cover after their passing.

3. Control and Timing: Individuals have the flexibility to choose when and how to distribute their wealth, allowing them to see the benefits of their gifts during their lifetime.

Strategies for Maximizing the Lifetime Gift Tax Exemption

1. Early Gifting: One effective strategy is to make gifts early in one's life. This strategy not only takes advantage of the tax exemption now but also ensures that any future increase in the value of these assets won't be taxed, which boosts overall tax savings.

2. Gift Appreciating Assets: By giving away assets like stocks or property that are likely to grow in value, you can take full advantage from the exemption benefits. The future appreciation occurs outside of the donor's estate, thereby reducing the potential estate tax.

3. Spousal Splitting: When married couples combine their exemptions, they can essentially increase the amount they can give without taxes, effectively doubling the tax-free allowance. This strategy, known as gift splitting, allows spouses to amplify their financial impact and further reduce their combined taxable estate.

4. Utilize Trusts: Trusts can be an excellent vehicle for utilizing the lifetime exemption. For instance, by placing assets in a bypass trust or a dynasty trust, people can not only decrease their taxable estate but also set terms for how assets are managed and distributed after their death.

5. Integrate with Business Succession Plans: For business owners, leveraging the lifetime exemption within a succession plan can facilitate a seamless change of ownership without significant tax liabilities.

Considerations and Limitations

1. Irrevocability: Gifts made under the lifetime exemption are irrevocable. Once the gift is done, the giver relinquishes control over these assets.

2. Potential Changes in Tax Law: Tax laws are subject to change. What works today may not be available in the future, so it's crucial to stay informed and be prepared to adjust strategies accordingly.

3. Documentation and Valuation: Accurate recording and evaluation of gifted assets are incredibly important. These records must withstand IRS scrutiny, particularly when gifting assets that are not easily valued, such as closely held business interests or unique personal property.

Utilizing the Annual Gift Tax Exclusion

As already discussed earlier, one straightforward and powerful approach for managing estate size and potential tax liabilities is through the use of the annual gift tax exclusion.

Each year, the annual gift tax exclusion in the U.S. tax code lets people transfer a specified sum of money or property to another individual without activating a gift tax or affecting their lifetime gift and estate tax allowance. As of 2024, the allowance amount is $18k per beneficiary. This lets a person to gift up to $18k annually to as many individuals as desired, these gifts will not being taxed or counting against their lifetime exemption of $13.61 million.

Benefits of the Annual Gift Tax Exclusion

1. Tax Savings: The primary benefit of utilizing the annual gift tax exclusion is the potential tax savings. By diminishing the magnitude of an estate, an individual can decrease the estate tax burden on their heirs might need to pay upon their passing.

2. Flexibility: The exclusion offers flexibility as it applies annually to each recipient. Therefore, a person can strategically gift assets to family members, friends, or even employees without triggering a taxable event.

3. Estate Reduction: Consistent, strategic use of the gift tax exclusion can substantially shrink an estate's size, potentially lowering it below the federal estate tax threshold.

How to Use the Annual Gift Tax Exclusion Effectively

1. Plan Early: Begin planning how to use the exclusion early. Consistent annual gifting can be a cornerstone of estate reduction strategies.

2. Use for Tuition and Medical Expenses: In addition to the $18,000 yearly exclusion, if you pay tuition directly to a school or healthcare costs directly to a healthcare provider, those expenditures won't be included in the $18,000 limit. This can be particularly effective for grandparents looking to support their grandchildren's education (more details later).

3. Gift Appreciating Assets: Think about transferring assets expected to increase in worth, like stocks or real estate. By transferring ownership, you're not just losing the asset's current value from your estate; you're also forfeiting any potential future increase in its worth.

4. Document Everything: Keep thorough records of all gifts made under this exclusion, including recipient details, relationship, amount, and date. This documentation will be crucial for tax purposes and estate settlement.

Considerations and Limitations

1. Impact on Beneficiary: Consider the potential financial impact on the beneficiary, including any implications for their eligibility for government benefits, financial aid, or their personal tax situation.

2. Irrevocability: Gifts made under the annual exclusion are irrevocable. Upon transfer, the assets are no longer controlled by the giver.

3. Marital Gifting Strategies: Married couples can merge their exclusions, allowing them to give up to $36,000 to one recipient without triggering a gift tax, thereby doubling the effectiveness of their gifting approach.

4. Coordination with Estate Plan: Ensure that annual gifting strategies are coordinated with the broader goals and tools of your estate plan, such as trusts or charitable donations.

Direct Payments for Medical and Educational Expenses

Paying specifically for another person's medical and educational expenses offers a valuable tax-saving strategy in estate planning that works alongside annual gift tax exclusions. Here's how it works:

Medical Expenses: The IRS allows you to pay for another person's medical expenses without any limit, only in case the funds are paid straight to the medical facility. These payments are not included in your annual gift tax allowance or your lifetime gift allowance. It's important that these payments cover expenses not reimbursed by insurance, including costs like hospital care, outpatient services, and some long-term care services.

Educational Expenses: Similar to medical payments, you can pay an unlimited amount of someone else's tuition expenses without triggering the gift tax. However, this exemption covers only tuition, excluding books, supplies, housing, and other educational expenses. Like medical expenses, payments must be made directly to the school.

Benefits of This Strategy

1. Unlimited Exclusion: Unlike the yearly gift tax exclusion, limiting the tax-free amount you can gift to any one individual per year ($18,000 in 2024), direct payments for medical and educational expenses are not limited. This allows you to provide substantial support without using any of your gift tax or estate tax exemptions.

2. Simplicity and Flexibility: This strategy does not require the setup of trusts or the administration associated with other estate planning tools. It offers a straightforward way to support loved ones, such as grandchildren or aging parents, ensuring their critical financial needs are met.

3. Immediate Impact: By directly paying for these expenses, you provide immediate benefit to the recipients, helping to relieve their financial burdens in real time. This is particularly meaningful in cases of sudden medical issues or for supporting ongoing education goals.

This strategy requires meticulous adherence to IRS rules—specifically ensuring that payments are made directly to institutions—to avoid unwanted taxes. It's advised to keep detailed records of all transactions to substantiate these payments in case of IRS scrutiny. Always consider consulting with a tax counselor or financial advisor to make sure that these payments are made in compliance with tax laws and align with your broader financial and estate planning goals.

Optimizing Estate Planning Through Charitable Contributions

Charitable contributions are not only a means to support meaningful causes but also an effective strategy for optimizing tax implications within estate planning. When integrated into estate planning, involves donating assets to charitable organizations either during an individual's lifetime or as a bequest in a will. These contributions can take various forms, such as cash donations, stocks, real estate, or other valuable assets.

Tax Benefits of Charitable Contributions

1. Estate Tax Reduction: A key advantage of making charitable donations is the possible reduction in estate taxes. Every dollar gifted to charity reduces the estate's size, thereby decreasing the potential estate tax liability.

2. Income Tax Deductions: Charitable contributions can provide significant income tax deductions. For example, donations to qualified charities may be deductible up to 60% of the donor's adjusted gross income (AGI) for cash donations and 30% for donations of appreciated assets like securities.

3. Avoidance of Capital Gains Tax: Donating assets that have increased in value, like stocks, houses etc. allows the donor to avoid capital gains taxes that would have been incurred if the assets were sold outright. The charity can then sell these assets without incurring these taxes, leveraging the full value of the donation.

Strategies for Integrating Charitable Giving into Estate Planning

1. Charitable Bequests: Including charitable gifts in your will is a straightforward method to reduce the taxable estate. Bequests can be designated as a fixed dollar amount, a fraction of the estate, or a residue after other bequests are made to heirs.

2. Charitable Trusts that can be sued (introduced before) are of two main categories:

   - Charitable Remainder Trusts (CRTs): This option lets you place your assets into a trust, ensuring you receive a regular income either for your lifetime or a specific amount of years. Afterward the trust's residual assets are transferred to the selected charity.

   - Charitable Lead Trusts (CLTs): Conversely, a CLT provides that the charity receives a regular income stream for a certain time, subsequently, the leftover assets return to the donor or beneficiaries. This approach can greatly lower the taxes heirs have to pay on gifts and inheritance of assets.

3. Donor-Advised Funds (DAFs): DAFs are an more and more common instrument for tax-effective charitable contribution. Donors have the opportunity to contribute to DAF and get a tax deduction right away for their charitable contribution. They have the ability to suggest which charities should receive grants from the fund over a period of time.

4. Gifts of Life Insurance: Gifting a life insurance policy to a charity can offer an immediate income tax deduction equivalent to the policy's cash surrender value. If the person donating keeps paying the insurance premiums, those payments might also qualify for tax deductions.

Considerations and Challenges

1. Documentation and Valuation: Proper documentation and valuation are crucial for tax reporting purposes. Appraisals may be necessary for non-cash donations, particularly for higher-value items.

2. Legal and Financial Advice: Given the complexities involved in setting up charitable donations through trusts or other means, consulting with legal and financial professionals is recommended to ensure adherence with tax laws and alignment with personal financial goals.

3. Long-Term Impact on Estate: Donors must think about the long-term implications of reducing their estate through charitable giving, particularly how it affects the inheritance of heirs.

Leveraging Portability in Estate Tax Planning

Portability is a relatively recent but profoundly impactful concept that can help married couples optimize their estate taxes. Introduced in 2011, portability means that upon the death of one spouse, the surviving partner can take advantage of any portion of the deceased spouse's federal estate and gift tax exemption that wasn't used. If one spouse doesn't utilize their full $13.61 million allowance (as of 2024), the unexploited part can be moved to the surviving partner, effectively allowing the couple to pass on up to $27.22 million to heirs without incurring federal estate tax.

How Portability Works

To understand how portability can be utilized effectively, it's important to grasp its mechanics. Here's a breakdown:

1. Election: Portability is not automatic. It requires filing a federal estate tax return (Form 706) at the first spouse's death, regardless of tax liability.

2. Exemption Amount: The total amount of exemption that can be transferred to the surviving spouse is known as the Deceased Spousal Unused Exclusion (DSUE). This amount plus the surviving spouse's own exemption can be used for lifetime gifts or transfers at death.

3. Timing: The election must be made within nine months after the death, although an extension of six months can be granted if requested before the due date.

Benefits of Using Portability

Portability offers several key benefits that can significantly enhance your estate planning strategy:

1. Simplicity: Compared to other tax optimization strategies, portability is relatively straightforward to implement, requiring primarily the timely filing of an estate tax return upon the death of the first spouse.

2. Flexibility: It provides the surviving spouse granting them more flexibility in structuring their own estate, allowing them to count on having a larger combined exemption amount.

3. Protection from Future Changes: Given that estate tax laws and exemption amounts can change, portability can offer some protection against reduction in exemption levels in the future. The surviving partner can claim the unexploited exemption of their passed partner/spouse, safeguarding it from potential legislative reductions.

Tax Optimization Scenarios

Let's consider some scenarios where portability can play a crucial role in tax planning:

1. Uneven Asset Distribution: Often, one spouse may hold significantly more assets in their name. Portability ensures that no matter which spouse dies first, the couple can fully utilize both exemptions.

2. Unexpected Deaths: If a spouse dies unexpectedly without having used their exemption, portability allows the couple to still take advantage of the unused portion, ensuring that careful planning does not go to waste.

3. Rising Asset Values: If the value of the surviving spouse's assets increases significantly, having access to a higher combined exemption can result in substantial tax savings upon their death.

While portability is a powerful tool, it should be considered alongside the potential use of trusts especially for issues like asset protection, managing how and when heirs receive their inheritance, and state estate tax concerns, as portability only applies to federal estate taxes.

Maximizing Step-Up in Basis

The step-up in basis is a tax provision that adjusts the value of an inherited asset for tax purposes upon the death of the owner. Instead of the heirs incurring capital gains tax calculated from the asset's original purchase price, the taxes are based on the asset's worth at the moment of the owner's passing. This adjustment can lead to substantial tax benefits, especially for highly appreciated assets.

Imagine you inherit a house that was purchased by a relative decades ago for $100,000, which is now worth $500,000. Without the step-up in basis, you would be liable for capital gains tax on $400,000 if you sold the house. When you inherit property, the taxable amount can reset to its current market value at inheritance due to a step-up in basis. This adjustment could lower or completely remove the capital gains tax you'd owe if you sell the property at that inherited value.

Strategies to Maximize Step-Up in Basis

1. Hold onto Appreciating Assets: If you own assets that are likely to increase in price, consider holding onto them until your death to allow your heirs to benefit from a step-up in basis. This approach is especially beneficial for real estate, stocks, or art.

2. Review and Reassess Your Portfolio: Regularly review your estate's portfolio to identify which assets are likely to appreciate and strategize your estate planning accordingly. Seeking advice from a financial expert can offer valuable perspectives tailored to your specific situation.

3. Consider Joint Ownership: For married couples, owning property jointly can allow the surviving spouse to receive a step-up in basis on the entire property, not just half of it, under certain conditions. This depends largely on the state's laws regarding property and inheritance.

4. Use a Trust Appropriately: Certain types of trusts can be used to facilitate a step-up in basis. For example, a revocable trust might be structured to include provisions that allow for assets to receive a step-up in basis upon the death of the trustor.

Real-World Application and Case Studies

Assuming the case of a family who inherited a set of stocks valued at $2 million, originally purchased for $500,000. Due to the step-up in basis rule, the family could sell the stocks shortly after inheriting them without incurring a significant capital gains tax, effectively saving them hundreds of thousands of dollars.

Potential Pitfalls and How to Avoid Them

1. Documentation and Record-Keeping: Ensure that all financial records are precise and current to substantiate the basis of assets at the time of inheritance. Poor record-keeping can lead to challenges in proving the stepped-up basis.

2. Navigating State Laws: Not all states handle the step-up in basis in the same way, especially in community property states. Grasping the nuances of your state's laws is essential and how they interact with federal tax laws.

3. Timing and Market Conditions: The value of an asset for step-up purposes is determined at the date of death or sometimes at an alternative valuation date six months later. Deciding whether to sell or hold an asset can depend heavily on market conditions at these times.

Utilizing Family Limited Partnerships (FLPs)

A Family Limited Partnership (FLP) is a strategic tool used in estate planning to manage and protect family assets while providing significant tax benefits. FLPs involve relatives combining their assets into a partnership for joint management. This arrangement not only facilitates the centralized management of assets but also helps in reducing estate and gift taxes, making it a favored strategy among families with considerable assets.

An FLP is structured where family members are typically general partners and limited partners. General partners oversee the partnership and make all investment and management decisions. Limited partners, however, do not engage in managing the assets and are not personally responsible beyond their investment. The key in FLPs is that the general partners can retain control over the assets, even though they may own only a small portion of the partnership's equity.

Tax Benefits of FLPs

1. Gift Tax Savings: A key advantage of an FLP is the capacity to pass wealth to the next generations while reducing gift and estate tax burdens. When family members have ownership in the Family Limited Partnership (FLP), the worth of these stakes can be significantly reduced due to factors like limited marketability and minority ownership. This allows the senior family members to transfer assets at a reduced value, which utilizes less of their gift tax exemption.

2. Estate Tax Reduction: FLPs can also support in optimizing estate taxes. Transferring assets into an FLP and incrementally gifting FLP interests to relatives allows the senior generation to reduce their taxable estate's value over time.

3. Asset Protection: Assets within an FLP benefit from a good level of protection from the creditors of the partners, provided that the FLP is structured and operated properly. This can be crucial for preserving wealth across generations.

Implementing FLPs for Tax Optimization

1. Formation and Funding: Establishing an FLP typically starts with legal documentation, including a partnership agreement. Assets such as real estate, investment accounts, or family businesses are then transferred into the FLP.

2. Valuation Discounts: Once the FLP is established, the interests held by family members often qualify for valuation discounts. These discounts are due to the limited marketability of FLP interests and the lack of control by limited partners, substantially lowering the taxable value of gifted interests.

3. Gifting Strategy: An effective strategy involves the senior family members gradually transferring FLP interests to family members, utilizing the annual gift tax exclusion, and leveraging valuation discounts to minimize overall gift tax exposure.

4. Compliance and Management: It's crucial for FLPs to be managed in compliance with legal standards and partnership agreements to ensure they are not disregarded by the IRS for tax purposes. Proper records, regular meetings, and formal minutes help establish the legitimacy of the FLP.

Considerations and Challenges

1. Legal and Professional Fees: Setting up and maintaining an FLP can involve significant legal and professional fees. It's key to balance these costs against the possible tax savings.

2. IRS Scrutiny: FLPs are closely scrutinized by the IRS, especially concerning valuation discounts and the operation of the partnership. It's incredibly key to show that every transaction is genuine and properly recorded.

3. Family Dynamics: Since FLPs involve close family collaboration, they can be impacted by family relationships and dynamics. Open communication and mutual agreements are vital to avoiding conflicts.

Strategic Integration of Retirement Accounts

Retirement holdings, like for example IRAs and 401(k)s, play a pivotal role in personal financial landscapes and estate planning due to their significant tax implications and potential growth over time. Strategically managing these accounts can substantially enhance the value passed on to heirs or chosen beneficiaries, including charitable organizations.

Retirement accounts are unique in estate planning due to their tax-deferred growth and specific tax treatment upon withdrawal. Traditional IRAs and 401(k)s, for instance, are taxed as ordinary income upon distribution, whereas Roth IRAs and Roth 401(k)s grow tax-free, with distributions typically made tax-free if certain conditions are met.

Naming Charitable Organizations as Beneficiaries

1. Tax Efficiency: Leaving retirement account assets to a charity offers significant tax efficiency. Charities are tax-exempt entities and can receive the full value of the account without owing income taxes on distributions, which maximizes the impact of your donation.

2. Simplifying Estate Liquidity: By naming a charity as a beneficiary of a retirement account, you can minimize your taxable estate, potentially lowering estate tax liabilities while contributing to a cause important to you.

Roth Conversions for Family Beneficiaries

1. Conversion Benefits: Switching a standard IRA or 401(k) to a Roth IRA encompasses paying income tax on the converted sum in the year of the conversion. However, this strategy can significantly benefit heirs because withdrawals from a Roth IRA are tax-free if the account has been open for at least five years and the owner is at least 59½ years old.

2. Long-Term Advantage: While the upfront tax cost of a Roth conversion can be substantial, the long-term benefits for your heirs are considerable. They will not only inherit assets free of income tax but also benefit from potential growth tax-free, which can be a crucial consideration in estate planning.

Strategic Considerations for Retirement Account Beneficiaries

1. Minimizing Income Taxes: When planning which assets to leave to heirs, consider their income tax situations. Heirs in higher tax brackets might benefit more from receiving Roth accounts, whereas those in lower brackets might be better suited to inherit traditional accounts.

2. Required Minimum Distributions (RMDs): Understanding the implications of RMDs is essential. Heirs are generally required to take mandatory withdrawals from inherited retirement accounts, which are taxable. Planning how these distributions will impact the overall taxation of the estate can be crucial.

3. Utilizing the Stretch IRA Strategy: Although recent changes in the law have limited the stretch IRA strategy (where beneficiaries could stretch distributions and the tax implications over their lifetimes), there are still planning opportunities, especially for eligible designated beneficiaries.

Case Studies and Practical Applications

1. Charitable Bequest: John, a retiree, designated a wildlife conservation charity as the beneficiary of his $500,000 IRA. Upon John's passing, the charity received the entire amount tax-free, utilizing these funds entirely for conservation efforts.

2. Roth Conversion Example: Sarah, anticipating substantial estate taxes, converted her traditional IRA to a Roth IRA, disbursing the taxes from her current non-retirement assets. Her children, both in high-income tax brackets, inherited the Roth IRA, benefiting from tax-free withdrawals, which offered them flexibility and reduced their tax burden.

Considerations on State-Specific Strategies

Estate planning is profoundly influenced by state-specific laws and regulations, which can vary dramatically across the United States. Understanding these nuances is crucial for optimizing estate tax liabilities and ensuring your estate plan aligns with local legal frameworks. This chapter delves into strategies that are tailored to the specific requirements and opportunities presented by different state laws.

Each state may have distinct regulations concerning estate and inheritance taxes, property laws, and even marital property rights. These differences mean that estate planning strategies effective in one state may not be suitable or even legal in another. Tailoring your estate planning to fit state-specific laws ensures compliance and maximizes tax efficiency.

Key Areas of State-Specific Consideration

1. Estate and Inheritance Taxes: As previously mentioned, certain states impose their own estate taxes, some have inheritance taxes, and a few exercise both or neither. For example, states like New Jersey and Maryland impose inheritance taxes, which can affect how you structure bequests.

2. Marital Property Laws: States differ in how they treat property owned by married couples, with distinctions between community property states and common law states. This impacts how property is valued and divided in an estate plan.

3. Homestead Exemptions: In several states, there's a homestead exemption designed to safeguard part of a home's value from creditors and legal processes like probate. The size and scope of these exemptions vary, impacting decisions about primary residences in estate planning.

4. Probate and Trust Laws: State laws dictate the probate process and the use of trusts. Some states have adopted the Uniform Probate Code, which simplifies and standardizes probate, while others have unique procedures that might complicate or streamline the process.

5. Gift Taxes: While most states follow federal guidelines regarding gift taxes, it's crucial to verify any state-specific regulations or exemptions that may apply to your gifting strategy.

Strategies for State-Specific Estate Planning

1. Utilize Trusts: In states with high estate taxes, explore establishing various trusts that can assist minimize state tax exposure. For example, bypass trusts or credit shelter trusts can be particularly useful in states where the state estate tax exemption is lower than the federal exemption.

2. Maximize Homestead Exemptions: In states with generous homestead exemptions, structuring property ownership to maximize these exemptions can protect a significant value of the estate from taxes and creditors.

3. Joint Tenancy Considerations: In community property states, converting property to joint tenancy might offer benefits like a double step-up in basis, minimizing taxes on the increased value of the property if sold after the death of one spouse.

4. Gifts and Annual Exclusions: Tailor your annual gifting strategies to align with state laws, particularly in states that have their own gift tax or where state laws might affect the tax consequences of those gifts.

5. State-Specific Vehicles: Some states offer unique estate planning vehicles or allowable deductions to minimize the total taxable estate. For instance, certain states might offer tax incentives for contributions to state-specific college savings plans or for investing in state bonds.

Electing Special Use Valuation for Family Farms and Businesses

Managing the tax implications of large asset valuations, especially for family farms and businesses, is crucial. One beneficial strategy is electing Special Use Valuation, which allows for the valuation of these assets based on their current use rather than their highest market value.

Special Use Valuation is a tax provision under Section 2032A of the Internal Revenue Code that permits a lower tax valuation of a farm or business property in an estate. This option is specifically designed to prevent the sale of farms and businesses due to high estate tax burdens at the time of the owner's death.

Eligibility and Requirements

To qualify for Special Use Valuation, several criteria must be met:

1. Type of Property: The property must be actively used for farming or a closely held business at the time of the owner's death.

2. Ownership and Operation: The decedent must have been a U.S. citizen or resident, and the property must have been owned and operated by the decedent or a family member for at least five years prior to death.

3. Gross Estate Limitation: The farm or business property must constitute at least 50% of the total gross estate and the qualified real property must be at least 25% of the gross estate.

4. Post-Death Requirements: Heirs are required to continue operating the farm or business in a similar manner for a period of at least ten years after the decedent's death to avoid penalties and potential recapture of the tax benefits.

Benefits of Special Use Valuation

1. Lower Estate Taxes: By allowing the property to be valued based on its agricultural or business use rather than its potential development value, taxes can be substantially reduced, easing financial burdens on the heirs.

2. Preservation of Family Enterprises: This provision helps ensure that family-owned farms and businesses can be passed down to the next generation without the need to sell or heavily mortgage the property to pay estate taxes.

Strategic Considerations

1. Estate Planning Integration: Electing Special Use Valuation should be integrated into a broader estate planning strategy, including wills, trusts, and succession planning, to ensure all elements work cohesively.

2. Long-Term Commitment: Heirs need to be prepared for the long-term commitment required to maintain the property's use as specified. This involves not only operational continuity but also potential legal obligations and reporting to the IRS.

3. Potential for Recapture: If the heirs fail to meet the requirements, such as changing the use of the property or selling it within the specified period, the IRS may recapture the taxes initially saved, plus interest and penalties.

Case Studies

Illustrative examples can help underscore the value of Special Use Valuation. For instance, consider a family whose farm was appraised at $5 million based on its development value but was eligible for Special Use Valuation at $2 million. This adjustment could save the family over a considerable amount in estate taxes, securing the farm's operation for another generation.

Section 23: Use of Life Insurance

When you consider the future and the legacy you want to leave behind, life insurance emerges as a powerful tool in your estate planning arsenal. It's about much more than just providing a death benefit; it's a strategic asset that can be instrumental in maintaining financial stability and continuity for your business and your family.

When you pass away, your estate might face significant financial demands, from paying estate taxes to covering outstanding debts and operating expenses for your business. Life insurance offers a source of immediate liquidity to meet these needs without the necessity to sell off assets at potentially unfavorable times. This liquidity ensures that your estate can cover these costs efficiently, preserving the value of the business and the assets you pass on to your heirs.

Life insurance can provide for your family's immediate and future financial needs, from helping to maintain their standard of living to ensuring that funds are available for future expenses like college tuition for your children. This benefit is especially important if your family relies on the income from your business. Life insurance can also be the funding mechanism for business buy-sell agreements because it provides the necessary capital exactly when it's needed. Upon the death of you or a co-owner, the life insurance policy disburses a death benefit to purchase the deceased owner's share of the business. This process eliminates the necessity for the remaining owners to use personal funds or business funds to buy out your interest, maintaining stability and liquidity in the business.

How to Integrate Life Insurance into Your Estate Plan

Integrating life insurance into your estate plan requires careful consideration and a strategic approach. Here's how you can think about incorporating life insurance based on your specific needs:

Assess Your Needs

Start by assessing the financial needs your family and business would face if you were no longer there. Consider:

- How much income would your family need to maintain their current lifestyle?

- How much capital would your business need to continue operating smoothly?

- What are the expected estate taxes and other obligations that will need to be taken care of?

Choose the Right Type of Life Insurance

Diverse categories of life insurance can serve different purposes in your estate plan:

- Term Life Insurance is straightforward and cost-effective, providing a death benefit if you pass away during the term of the policy. It's a good choice if your need for insurance is temporary or if you seek an affordable method to support specific liabilities that diminish over time, such as a mortgage or business loan.

- Whole Life and Universal Life Insurance are types of permanent life insurance policies that not only provide a death benefit but also include a cash value component that grows over time. These policies can be more expensive but offer additional flexibility and can be part of more complex estate planning strategies, such as funding a trust or providing lifelong financial support for a dependent with special needs.

Coordinate with Other Estate Planning Tools

Life insurance should work in concert with the rest of your estate plan. For illustration:

- If you have established trusts as part of your estate plan, life insurance can provide the funds to be held in trust for your beneficiaries, ensuring that the proceeds are managed according to your wishes.

- If you are using life insurance to fund a buy-sell agreement, make sure the beneficiaries are properly designated and the amount aligns with the valuation of your business interest.

Your financial situation and your business will evolve, and so should your estate plan. Consistently reassess your life insurance to confirm it aligns with your current needs and make adjustments as necessary. This might mean increasing coverage as your business grows or adjusting your strategy if your family's needs change.

While life insurance is a powerful tool, it's important to be aware of common pitfalls:

- Underestimating Your Needs: It's easy to underestimate the amount of life insurance you need to cover all potential expenses and ensure your family and business are adequately provided for.

- Policy Ownership Issues: The way a life insurance policy is owned can affect the tax treatment of the proceeds. Ensure the policy ownership aligns with your broader estate planning objectives to prevent creating additional tax liabilities.

- Failing to Keep Beneficiaries Updated: As life changes, so might your choice of beneficiaries. Regular updates ensure that the death benefit from your life insurance goes to the intended recipients.

Section 24: Balancing Growth and Protection in Estate Planning

Estate planning is a delicate balance between growing your wealth and protecting it. While it's crucial to maximize the potential growth of your assets, it's equally important to safeguard them against risks that could erode your wealth. Achieving this balance requires strategic planning and a comprehensive understanding of various financial instruments and legal structures.

Balancing growth and protection in estate planning involves developing strategies that allow your wealth to grow while ensuring that it is protected from potential threats. These threats can include market volatility, legal disputes, taxes, and creditor claims. By implementing a well-rounded estate plan, you can achieve financial security and make sure that your legacy is preserved for the next generations.

Strategic Asset Allocation

One of the foundational principles of balancing growth and protection is strategic asset allocation. This involves diversifying investments across different asset types like stocks, bonds, real estate, and other investments. Diversification helps manage risk by mitigating the effect of any single investment's poor results on your entire portfolio.

When creating your estate plan, think about how each type of investment might grow and the risks involved. Stocks and real estate can offer significant growth opportunities but come with higher volatility. Bonds and other fixed-income securities provide more stability but may offer lower returns. By balancing these assets, you can build a portfolio that matches your risk appetite and financial objectives.

Tax-Efficient Investment Strategies

Minimizing taxes is essential for safeguarding your wealth and maximizing growth. Implementing tax-efficient investment strategies can strongly influence the long-term value of your estate. This includes utilizing tax-favored accounts such as IRAs, 401(k)s, and Roth IRAs, that benefit from tax advantages enhancing the growth of your assets.

Additionally, evaluate the tax consequences of your investment decisions. For instance, holding investments for the long term might qualify for lower applicable taxes, while utilizing tax-loss harvesting can counterbalance gains with losses, lowering your total tax burden. Consulting with a tax counselor can help you identify and implement these strategies effectively.

Section 25: General Considerations for Various Asset Types in Estate Planning

Estate planning involves making critical decisions about a diverse range of assets. Each asset type has unique characteristics and requires specific considerations to ensure they are managed and transferred effectively. This comprehensive guide explores the nuances of estate planning for various asset types, including real estate, financial assets, art and collectibles, digital assets, and unconventional assets. By understanding these considerations, you can produce a comprehensive estate plan that aligns to your objectives and safeguards your legacy.

Real Estate in Estate Planning

Real estate is frequently one of the most significant components of an estate, and it requires careful planning to manage and transfer effectively. Real estate includes primary residences, vacation homes, rental properties, and commercial buildings. Each type of property comes with its own set of legal, financial, and tax implications.

When planning for real estate, it's essential to consider the current market value, potential appreciation, and associated costs such as maintenance, taxes, and insurance. A detailed valuation of your real estate assets provides a clear picture of their worth and helps in making informed decisions about their disposition.

One popular approach to handling real estate in estate planning is setting up trusts. Placing real estate in a trust will help circumvent probate, provide privacy, and guarantee the property is managed as per your directives. A revocable living trust, for instance, lets you keep control over the property while you are alive and specifies how it must be managed and allocated after your passing.

If you own rental or commercial properties, succession planning becomes crucial. This involves designating a successor to manage the properties and ensuring they have the necessary skills and resources to do so effectively. You may also consider creating a family limited partnership (FLP) or a limited liability company (LLC) to hold the real estate. These structures can offer liability protection and facilitate the transfer of ownership to your heirs while minimizing tax liabilities.

Financial Assets in Estate Planning

Financial assets encompass a big variety of holdings, including bank accounts, investment portfolios, retirement accounts, and life insurance policies. Each type of financial asset has unique considerations for estate planning, particularly regarding tax implications and beneficiary designations.

Bank accounts and investment portfolios should have designated beneficiaries to ensure a smooth transfer of assets upon your death. Payable-on-death (POD) and transfer-on-death (TOD) designations can help bypass the probate process, allowing beneficiaries to access funds quickly.

Retirement accounts, such as IRAs and 401(k)s, require special attention due to their tax-deferred status. Naming the right beneficiaries is crucial, as different rules apply to spousal and non-spousal beneficiaries. A spousal beneficiary can roll over the account into their own IRA, while non-spousal beneficiaries must follow specific distribution rules that can affect the tax treatment of the inherited funds.

Life insurance policies are another critical component of financial assets in estate planning. The proceeds from life insurance can provide liquidity to cover estate taxes, debts, and other expenses, ensuring that your heirs receive their inheritance without financial strain. To maximize the benefits, consider setting up an irrevocable life insurance trust (ILIT), which removes the policy from your taxable estate and provides additional asset protection.

Art and Collectibles in Estate Planning

Art and collectibles, including fine art, antiques, jewelry, and rare items, present unique challenges in estate planning due to their value, emotional significance, and market volatility. Properly managing these assets requires accurate valuation, careful documentation, and strategic planning.

The valuation of art and collectibles can be complex, as their market value can fluctuate significantly. It's key to get professional appraisals from competent experts to estimate their current worth. These appraisals should be updated regularly to reflect changes in the market.

Documenting the provenance and condition of each item is crucial for maintaining their value and facilitating their transfer. Detailed records, including purchase receipts, appraisal reports, and historical information, can help establish authenticity and enhance the value of the assets.

When planning for the transfer of art and collectibles, consider the tax implications. Selling these assets may incur capital gains taxes, and they might also face estate tax obligations when they are passed on. Gifting items during your lifetime, either to family members or charitable organizations, can help reduce the taxable value of your estate. Establishing a charitable remainder trust (CRT) lets you give valuable assets to charity while benefiting from proceeds and possible tax advantages.

Digital Assets in Estate Planning

In today's digital age, digital assets have become an integral part of estate planning. Digital assets include online accounts, social media profiles, digital currencies, and intellectual property. Managing these assets requires understanding their unique characteristics and ensuring that your estate plan addresses their transfer and management.

First, identify and catalog all your digital assets. This includes listing online banking accounts, email accounts, social media profiles, and any digital investments such as cryptocurrencies. Providing detailed instructions on how to access these accounts, including usernames, passwords, and security questions, is essential for ensuring that your executor or designated representative can manage them effectively.

Next, consider the legal aspects of transferring digital assets. Many online platforms have specific terms of service that govern the transfer of accounts upon death. Reviewing these terms and making necessary arrangements, such as designating a legacy contact or authorized representative, can help ensure a smooth transition.

For valuable digital assets, such as digital currencies or intellectual property, consider setting up a digital asset trust. This type of trust provides a legal framework for managing and transferring digital assets, ensuring that they are safeguarded and allocated as per your intentions.

Unconventional Assets in Estate Planning

Unconventional assets encompass a broad range of holdings that may not fit neatly into traditional asset categories. These can include intellectual property rights, business interests, royalties, and other unique investments. Each type of unconventional asset requires specific considerations for effective estate planning.

Patents, trademarks, and copyrights, as forms of intellectual property, can possess substantial value and require specialized management. Ensure that these assets are properly documented and protected through appropriate legal channels. Think about establishing a trust to oversee these rights and provide clear instructions for their transfer and management.

Business interests, whether in a family-owned business or other ventures, require detailed succession planning. Establishing a clear plan for transferring ownership and management responsibilities can help ensure the continuity of the business and protect its value. Legal structures such as FLPs or LLCs can facilitate this transfer and provide additional tax benefits.

Royalties from books, music, or other creative works can provide a steady income stream for your heirs. Properly managing these assets involves ensuring that contracts and agreements are up to date and that royalties are correctly accounted for and distributed.

Section 26: Adapting Your Estate Plan Through Life's Stages

Estate planning is a dynamic process that evolves as you move through different stages of life. Your wishes, assets, and family situation can evolve significantly with time, requiring periodic updates to keep your estate plan in sync with your current situation and wishes. By understanding how to adapt your estate plan at each stage of life, you can safeguard your legacy and ensure your loved ones are provided for.

Early Adulthood: Building the Foundation

As you transition into early adulthood, estate planning might not seem like a priority, but it is essential to lay a solid foundation. At this stage, you may not have accumulated significant assets, but you should still consider creating basic estate planning documents. A will is a fundamental tool that enables you to dictate the distribution of your assets and who will manage your estate. Additionally, establishing a durable power of attorney and a healthcare proxy authorize a trusted individual to make financial and medical decisions for you if you become incapacitated.

Insurance is another critical component at this stage. Consider obtaining life insurance to provide financial support for any dependents you may have and to cover any debts, such as student loans or a mortgage. As you build your career and start to accumulate more assets, consistently reassessing and revising beneficiary designations on retirement accounts and life insurance policies is vital.

Starting a Family: Expanding Your Plan

When you start a family, your estate planning needs become more complex. Protecting your spouse and children becomes a primary concern. This is the time to update your will to include provisions for guardianship of your minor children. Naming a guardian in your will ensures that your children will be cared for by someone you trust if you and your spouse are no longer able to do so.

Establishing a trust can be a strong tool for administrating and safeguarding your children's inheritance. A trust lets you dictate the timing and manner of your assets' distribution, providing financial security for your children while they are still minors and ensuring that they receive the support they need for education and other expenses.

Life insurance becomes even more critical during this stage. Adequate life insurance coverage can provide a financial safety net for your family, covering living expenses, education costs, and other financial needs. Review your insurance policies regularly to confirm the coverage amount adequately meets your family's requirements.

Midlife: Managing Growth and Complexity

As you progress into midlife, your financial situation and estate planning needs may become more complex. You might have accumulated significant assets, such as a home, investments, and retirement accounts. At this stage, it's key to revise and amend your estate plan to align with these modifications.

Consider incorporating advanced estate planning strategies, like for example establishing a revocable living trust. A living trust can give you the possibility to manage your assets during your life and provide a seamless transition of your estate after your death, avoiding the lengthy and costly probate process. Additionally, a living trust offers more privacy than a will, as it does not become a public record.

If you have a business, planning for succession becomes vital aspect of your estate plan. Developing a clear succession plan makes sure that your business can keep operating smoothly in your absence. This might involve creating a buy-sell agreement, appointing a successor, and providing training and support to prepare them for their new role.

Pre-Retirement: Securing Your Future

As you approach retirement, your focus may shift towards ensuring that your estate plan provides for your long-term care and supports a smooth transition of assets to your heirs. This is the time to review your retirement accounts and make any necessary adjustments to your beneficiary designations. Verify that your estate plan complements your retirement objectives and provides for your financial security.

Long-term care planning is a crucial component at this stage. Think about acquiring long-term care insurance to manage possible healthcare expenses and protect your assets from being depleted by medical expenses. Additionally, review and update your healthcare directives and powers of attorney to ensure that your wishes are respected if you become incapacitated.

Updating your will and trust documents to reflect your current wishes and financial situation is essential. Ensure that your estate plan addresses any shifts in your family, like going through marriages, divorcing, or the arrival of grandchildren. Consistently revising and updating your estate plan prevents conflicts and guarantees your wishes are honored.

Retirement: Preserving Your Legacy

In retirement, your estate planning focus shifts towards maintaining your legacy and ensuring your assets are allocated as you desire. This is the time to review your estate plan and make any final adjustments to align it with your present situation and objectives.

Consider philanthropic goals and how they can be incorporated into your estate plan. Charitable giving strategies, like establishing a charitable remainder trust or initiating a donor-advised fund, can offer tax benefits while supporting causes that are important to you.

Review your trust and estate documents often to make sure that they remain current and relevant. Discuss your estate plan with your family to provide clarity and transparency, helping to prevent misunderstandings and disputes.

Section 27: Tailored Strategies 7 Key Scenarios

Estate planning is a highly personalized process that must be customized to align with each individual's specific circumstances and objectives. A universal solution does not exist when it comes to planning your estate. Different life situations require different methods to guarantee your wishes are honored and your assets are allocated per your specifications intentions. Let's explore several common scenarios and the tailored estate strategies that can address each one effectively.

Scenario 1: Young Families

As a young family, your primary concerns often revolve around ensuring that your children are cared for if something happens to you and that your spouse is financially secure. One of the most important elements of your estate plan should include naming a guardian for your minor children. This involves legally naming someone you trust to take care of your children if you are no longer able to do so. Additionally, establishing a trust can be a wise method to handle the financial support for your children's education and upbringing. Life insurance policies play a significant role here as well, providing a financial safety net to cover living expenses, education costs, and other necessities.

Scenario 2: Single Individuals with No Children

If you are a single individual without children, your estate planning needs will be different. You might focus more on guaranteeing your assets go to your designated beneficiaries, whether they are family members, friends, or charitable organizations. Creating a detailed will is crucial to outline your wishes clearly. Contemplate establishing a living trust to oversee your assets during your lifetime and ensure a seamless transition after your death. Powers of attorney for financial and healthcare decisions are also essential, ensuring that a trusted individual can act on your behalf if you become incapacitated.

Scenario 3: Blended Families

Blended families, where there are children from previous relationships, face unique challenges in estate planning. Crafting a plan is crucial that balances the needs and expectations of all family members. One effective strategy is to use a combination of wills and trusts to ensure that your spouse is provided for while also securing inheritances for your biological children. A qualified terminable interest property (QTIP) trust could bring advantages, enabling you to support your surviving spouse while safeguarding assets for your children from a previous marriage.

Scenario 4: Business Owners

For business owners, estate planning must address both personal and business assets. Succession planning is essential, guaranteeing your business can continue to operate smoothly in your absence. You might consider creating a buy-sell agreement, which outlines how your business interest will be transferred upon your death or incapacity. This agreement can provide a clear plan for the continuity of the business and prevent potential disputes among heirs or business partners. Additionally, trusts and other mechanisms serves to oversee and safeguard business assets, guaranteeing they are allocated per your intentions.

Scenario 5: Wealthy Individuals

Wealthy individuals often face more complex estate planning challenges, including reducing estate taxes and shielding assets from creditors. Utilizing a variety of trusts, such as irrevocable life insurance trusts (ILITs) and grantor retained annuity trusts (GRATs), can help reduce the taxable estate and provide liquidity to pay estate taxes. Charitable giving strategies, such as charitable remainder trusts (CRTs) and charitable lead trusts (CLTs), can also be effective in reducing tax liabilities while supporting your philanthropic goals. Asset protection strategies, including the use of family limited partnerships (FLPs), can further safeguard your wealth.

Scenario 6: Families with Special Needs Children

If you have a child with special needs, your estate plan must secure their long-term care while preserving their eligibility for government benefits. A special needs trust (SNT) is a critical tool in this scenario, allowing you to set aside funds for your child's care while preserving their access to essential benefits such as Medicaid and Supplemental Security Income (SSI). The SNT can be designed to cover expenses not provided by these programs, enhancing your child's quality of life.

Scenario 7: Retirees and Seniors

As a retiree or senior, your focus might be on ensuring that your plan addresses your healthcare needs and ensures a smooth transition of assets to your heirs. Long-term care planning, including securing long-term care insurance is essential to manage potential healthcare expenses. Updating your will and ensuring that your beneficiary designations on retirement accounts and life insurance policies are current is essential. Additionally, consider creating a living trust to direct your assets and bypass probate, a process that can be lengthy and expensive.

Section 28: Cross-Border Estate Planning: Navigating International Complexities

Whether you own property overseas, have financial accounts in multiple countries, or your heirs reside in different jurisdictions, a well-structured plan can help manage these complexities. Effective cross-border estate planning ensures that your assets are distributed according to your wishes, minimizes tax liabilities, and prevents legal disputes among heirs.

Navigating cross-border estates involves understanding different legal systems, tax implications, and logistical challenges. Each country has its own set of laws governing inheritance, estate taxes, and the validity of wills and trusts. Without careful planning, your estate could face significant hurdles, including double taxation, legal disputes, and delays in asset distribution.

Understanding Different Legal Systems

The legal frameworks governing estates can vary significantly, primarily falling into two broad categories: common law and civil law systems. Understanding these systems and their key differences is crucial for effective cross-border estate planning.

Common Law vs. Civil Law Systems

Legal systems around the world are generally classified into two main types: common law and civil law. Each system has its own principles and rules that can significantly impact estate planning.

Common law systems are based on legal precedents set by judicial decisions over time. These precedents, also known as case law, guide judges in making decisions on current cases. Common law is widely used in countries like the United States, the United Kingdom, Canada, Australia, and India.

In the context of estate planning, common law systems tend to offer more flexibility. For example, individuals generally have the freedom to distribute their assets as they see fit, without mandatory rules dictating who must inherit. This adaptability permits the utilization of diverse estate planning instruments, including wills, trusts, and powers of attorney, to tailor the allocation of assets per the individual's desires.

Civil law systems, in contrast, are based on codified statutes and laws rather than judicial precedents. This system is common in many countries across Europe, Asia, and Latin America, including France, Germany, Japan, and Brazil.

Estate planning under civil law systems is often more rigid due to "forced heirship" rules. These rules mandate that certain portions of an individual's estate must be allocated to specific family members, typically children and spouses. This legal obligation can limit an individual's ability to distribute their assets freely and may necessitate careful planning to comply with these statutory requirements while still achieving personal estate planning goals.

Key Differences in Estate Planning Laws

The distinctions between common law and civil law systems lead to several key differences in how estate planning is conducted.

Flexibility and Freedom of Disposition

One of the most significant differences is the degree of freedom individuals have in disposing of their assets. Common law systems generally allow greater freedom of disposition, enabling individuals to bequeath their assets to whomever they choose. This freedom is facilitated through the use of wills and trusts, which can be crafted to reflect the individual's specific wishes and objectives.

In contrast, civil law systems impose restrictions through forced heirship rules. These rules are designed to protect the rights of close family members, ensuring that a portion of the estate is reserved for them regardless of the deceased's wishes. For example, in France, a parent must leave a certain percentage of their estate to their children, depending on the number of children. This can significantly constrain the testator's ability to distribute their assets as they desire.

Use of Trusts

Trusts are another aspect where common law and civil law systems diverge. Trusts are a cornerstone of estate planning in common law countries. They allow to manage and protect assets, minimize taxes, and guarantee the testator's intentions are fulfilled efficiently. Trusts can be customized for numerous purposes, such as shielding assets from creditors, providing for minor children, and managing charitable donations.

In civil law countries, however, trusts are less common and often not as well-integrated into the legal system. Some civil law jurisdictions have adapted to recognize and enforce trusts, but the legal frameworks may still be less developed compared to common law countries. As a result, individuals in civil law countries may need to rely more on alternative estate planning instruments, like foundations or life insurance, to achieve similar goals.

Probate Process

The probate process, which involves validating and administering a deceased person's will, also varies between civil law systems and common law systems. Probate can be formal by common law, typically there is a court-supervised process that ensures the will is authentic and the estate is allocated according to the testator's directives. This process can sometimes be lengthy and costly, depending on the complexity of the estate and the jurisdiction's specific probate rules.

In civil law jurisdictions, the probate process tends to be more administrative and less judicial. The focus is often on ensuring compliance with forced heirship rules and other statutory requirements, rather than validating the will through a court process. This can make the administration of estates quicker and less expensive, but it also means that individuals have less flexibility in how their assets are distributed.

Tax Implications of Cross-Border Estates

Managing taxes is one of the most complex aspects of cross-border estate planning. When dealing with cross-border estates, it's key to comprehend the estate and inheritance tax laws in each relevant jurisdiction. Different countries have varying approaches to taxation at death, which can significantly impact the distribution of your assets.

Estate Taxes

As discussed before Estate taxes are imposed on the value of the departed person's estate before the assets are distributed to the heirs. Countries like the United States impose estate taxes on the worldwide assets of their citizens and residents. The U.S. estate tax exemption limit, which is adjusted annually for inflation, allows estates below a certain threshold to be exempt from taxation.

Inheritance Taxes

Inheritance taxes conversely are levied on the beneficiaries who receive the assets. Countries like the United Kingdom and Japan have inheritance taxes, which can vary based on the connection between the deceased and the beneficiary. Close relatives might receive preferential tax rates compared to more distant relatives or non-relatives.

Understanding whether a country imposes estate or inheritance taxes—or both—is critical for planning. This understanding allows you to structure your estate plan in a way that optimize the entire tax load on your heirs.

Tax Treaties and Double Taxation

Double taxation occurs when two countries levy taxes on the same income or assets. This can be a significant issue in cross-border estates, where both the country of residence and the country where assets are located might claim tax jurisdiction. To mitigate this, many countries have entered into tax treaties designed to prevent double taxation.

Tax Treaties

Tax treaties often include provisions that allocate taxing rights between the countries and provide relief from double taxation. These treaties can specify which country has the primary right to tax certain assets and may allow for tax credits to offset taxes paid in another country. For example, the U.S. has tax treaties with several countries, including the United Kingdom, Canada, and Germany, which provide mechanisms to avoid double taxation on estates and inheritances.

Double Taxation Relief

If there is no tax treaty between the countries involved, domestic laws might still provide some relief. Countries often have unilateral measures that allow for a credit or deduction for taxes paid to another country. This helps reduce the overall tax burden, although the specifics can vary widely between jurisdictions.

Strategies for Minimizing Tax Liabilities

Effective estate planning involves implementing strategies to minimize tax liabilities across multiple jurisdictions. Here are several approaches that can help minimize the tax effect on your estate.

Use of Trusts

Trusts are good tools in estate planning, offering both asset protection and tax benefits. Putting assets in a trust can potentially defend them from estate taxes and inheritance taxes. Trusts can be particularly useful in jurisdictions that recognize them for tax purposes, allowing you to take advantage of favorable tax treatment.

Gifting During Lifetime

Making gifts during your lifetime can decrease your estate's value and thus optimize the estate tax burden. Numerous countries offer annual gift tax exemptions, permitting the transfer of a specified sum or assets each year without suffering gift taxes. In the U.S., for example, the annual gift tax exclusion for 2024 is $17,000 per recipient. By systematically gifting assets, you can lower your estate's taxable value over time.

Charitable Donations

Charitable donations offers substantial tax advantages. Donations to eligible charitable organizations are often deductible, reducing the overall taxable value of your estate. Establishing Charitable trusts like Charitable Remainder Trusts (CRTs) or Charitable Lead Trusts (CLTs) offer continuous tax advantages while backing up your big-hearted goals.

Life Insurance

Life insurance offers a practical solution for providing liquidity to cover estate taxes, especially in countries with high estate tax rates. Proceeds from life insurance policies are generally free from income tax and can be structured to bypass estate tax if placed in an irrevocable life insurance trust (ILIT).

Double Taxation Agreements

Taking full advantage of double taxation agreements (DTAs) between countries can also minimize your tax liabilities. These agreements can assist you in organizing your estate so that reduces or eliminates double taxation. Consulting with an international tax advisor is crucial to navigating these agreements effectively.

Wills and Trusts in Cross-Border Planning

Drafting valid wills, utilizing trusts, and coordinating these documents across different countries are crucial steps in managing an international estate.

Drafting Valid Wills in Multiple Jurisdictions

When you have assets in multiple countries, it is essential to draft wills that comply with the legal requirements of each jurisdiction. A will that is valid in one country may not be recognized in another, leading to potential hinderances and postponements in settling your estate.

To confirm the validity of your wills, you might consider creating separate wills for each country where you hold significant assets. This method enables you to customize each will to the specific legal requirements and inheritance laws of that jurisdiction. However, it is crucial to coordinate these wills carefully to avoid conflicts and ensure that they work together seamlessly.

For example, if you have property in both the United States and France, you would need to draft a will for your U.S. assets that complies with American probate laws and another will for your French assets that adheres to French inheritance laws. Each will should include a revocation clause that clearly states it does not revoke the other will, preventing any unintended nullification.

The Role of Trusts in International Estates

In a cross-border context, trusts can help mitigate the complexities of different legal systems. For instance, placing assets in a trust can avoid the forced heirship rules common in civil law countries. These rules dictate that a certain portion of your estate must go to specific heirs, limiting your ability to distribute your assets freely. A trust can provide a way to manage these assets according to your terms while still complying with local laws.

Coordinating Multiple Wills and Trusts

Coordinating multiple wills and trusts is crucial to guarantee your estate plan functions harmoniously across different jurisdictions. Here are several strategies to achieve effective coordination:

1. Clear Delineation of Assets: Clearly specify which assets are governed by each will or trust. This helps avoid overlaps and ensures that each document only covers assets in its respective jurisdiction.

2. Consistent Legal Language: Use consistent language and terminology in all your estate planning documents. This reduces the risk of misinterpretation and ensures that your intentions are clear across different legal systems.

3. Professional Coordination: Work with estate planning attorneys in each relevant jurisdiction. These professionals can ensure that your documents comply with local laws and that all aspects of your estate plan are integrated effectively.

4. Centralized Communication: Maintain a central file or database that contains all your estate planning documents, along with contact information for all your advisors. This ensures that your executors and trustees can easily access the necessary information and coordinate their efforts.

5. Regular Reviews: Periodically review and update your estate planning documents to reflect any changes in your assets, family situation, or relevant laws. Regular reviews help keep your estate plan current and effective.

Asset Management and Transfer in Cross-Border Estates

Repatriating Assets

Repatriating assets involves transferring your foreign assets back to your home country. This process can be complex due to legal and tax implications. Here are some key considerations for repatriating assets:

Legal Compliance

Before repatriating assets, ensure that you comply with both the foreign country's laws and the laws of your home country. This might include obtaining necessary approvals or clearances from relevant authorities. Failing to meet these legal requirements can lead to penalties or legal disputes.

Tax Implications

Repatriating assets can trigger tax liabilities in both the foreign country and your home country. For example, transferring property or liquidating investments might result in capital gains tax. Understanding tax implications and planning strategically can reduce your tax liability. Consulting with international tax advisors is crucial to navigate these complexities effectively.

Financial Considerations

Transferring large sums of money or valuable assets across borders can involve significant financial costs, including transfer fees and currency exchange costs. It's crucial to account for these costs and strategize your repatriation strategy to minimize costs. This might involve transferring assets gradually over time or using financial instruments to hedge against currency fluctuations.

Documentation and Record-Keeping

Maintaining thorough documentation and records is essential when repatriating assets. This includes keeping track of all transactions, obtaining necessary approvals, and documenting the source of funds. Proper documentation can help you address any regulatory inquiries and ensure a smooth repatriation process.

Currency Considerations and Exchange Rates

Managing currency considerations and exchange rates is a critical aspect of cross-border estate planning. Variations in exchange rates can greatly affect the value of your assets and the efficiency of their transfer.

Currency Hedging

Currency hedging uses financial tools to guard against market volatility in currency conversation rates. This helps stabilize the value of your possessions and reduce the risk associated with currency movements. Popular hedging techniques include forward contracts, options, and swaps.

Diversification

Diversifying your assets across different currencies can help reduce the effects of currency volatility. This involves holding investments and accounts in multiple currencies, providing a natural hedge against exchange rate volatility. Diversification can also provide access to different financial markets and investment opportunities.

Timing of Transfers

The time at which the asset transfers are done can greatly affect the value you receive due to exchange rate fluctuations. Monitoring exchange rates and choosing the optimal time for transfers can help maximize the value of your repatriated assets. This might involve waiting for favorable exchange rates or spreading transfers over time to average out currency risks.

Legal and Financial Advisors in Cross-Border Estate Planning

International legal advisors play a pivotal role in cross-border estate planning. These professionals have specialized knowledge of the legal systems in multiple countries and can navigate the intricate laws that govern estate planning across borders.

One of their primary responsibilities is to ensure that your estate planning documents comply with the laws of all relevant jurisdictions. This involves drafting wills and trusts that are valid in each country where you hold assets or have beneficiaries. They can clarify the consequences of various legal systems, like the differences between common law and civil law, and how these impact your estate plan.

Additionally, international legal advisors can assist with the probate process in different countries, guaranteeing the management of your estate is done smoothly and in accordance with local laws. They can also help mitigate the effects of forced heirship rules in civil law countries by utilizing trusts or other legal structures that offer greater flexibility.

International financial advisors bring a wealth of expertise in managing cross-border financial issues. They can guide you through the intricate tax consequences of holding assets in multiple jurisdictions and devise strategies to minimize tax liabilities.

These advisors are skilled in creating tax-efficient estate plans that take advantage of international tax treaties and other mechanisms to prevent double taxation. They can also help manage currency risks and ensure that your assets are diversified across different currencies to mitigate exchange rate volatility.

In addition to tax planning, international financial advisors can assist with investment management, ensuring that your portfolio is in sync with your long-term objectives and risk tolerance, offering expert guidance on repatriating assets, managing financial accounts in multiple countries, and navigating the financial regulations of different jurisdictions.

Choosing the Right Professionals for Cross-Border Estates

Selecting the right legal and financial advisors is essential for effective cross-border estate planning. Consider these crucial factors when choosing professionals to assist with your international estate.

Expertise and Experience

Look for advisors who specialize in cross-border estate planning and have extensive experience working with clients who have international assets. They need to be well-versed in the legal and financial systems of the countries where your assets are located. Ask about their experience with similar cases and request references to ensure they have a proven track record of success.

Professional Credentials

Verify the credentials of potential advisors to ensure they are qualified to handle your estate planning needs. This includes checking their education, certifications, and professional affiliations. Legal advisors should be licensed to practice law in the relevant jurisdictions, while financial advisors should have pertinent credentials like Certified Financial Planner (CFP) or Chartered Financial Analyst (CFA).

Communication and Collaboration

Choose professionals who are responsive, communicate clearly, and are willing to work together to develop a cohesive estate plan. They must be capable to elucidate multifaceted legal and financial concepts in a form that you can comprehend and make well-versed decisions.

Tailored Advice

Your estate plan should be customized to fit your specific needs and objectives. Look for advisors who take the time to understand your situation and provide personalized advice. They should be proactive in identifying potential issues and offering solutions that meet your goals.

Fee Structure

Understand the fee structure of potential advisors before engaging their services. Some advisors charge hourly rates, while others may offer fixed fees or a percentage of the assets under management. Ensure that the fee structure is transparent and aligns with your budget and expectations.

Global Network

Consultants with a global network of contacts can provide additional value in cross-border estate planning. They can leverage their connections with other professionals, such as local lawyers and financial consultants, to guarantee every facet of your estate plan are addressed comprehensively. This network can be particularly beneficial in navigating the legal and financial intricacies of multiple jurisdictions.

|Part 6| Execution

Section 29: Choosing Between DIY and Professional Estate Planning Services

In estate planning, a decision you'll encounter early on is whether to do it yourself (DIY) or hire a professional. This choice can significantly impact the effectiveness, legality, and ease of implementing your estate plan.

What is DIY Estate Planning?

DIY estate planning involves personally creating legal instruments like wills, trusts, and power of attorney without the direct help of an estate planning attorney. This often involves using online software, templates, or guides to prepare these documents.

Pros of DIY Estate Planning:

1. Cost-Effective: Typically less expensive than hiring a professional. This can be appealing if you have a straightforward estate or a limited budget.

2. Convenience: You can work on your estate plan according to your own schedule and pace without needing to coordinate with a professional's availability.

3. Control: Some people prefer the direct control over the drafting and decision-making process that DIY options offer.

Cons of DIY Estate Planning:

1. Potential for Errors: Without professional guidance, there is a higher risk of making mistakes, which could be costly or problematic to rectify after your death.

2. Complexity Overlooked: DIY methods may not adequately address unique situations or more complex estates, potentially leading to oversights and vulnerabilities.

3. Lack of Legal Advice: DIY estate planning does not provide customized legal advice or insights that could be beneficial in optimizing your estate plan.

The Role of Professional Estate Planning Services

Professional estate planning services involve hiring qualified professionals, such as estate planning attorneys, to help create and manage your estate plan. These experts bring their knowledge of law, tax, and personal circumstances to guarantee that your estate plan is comprehensive and legally secure.

Pros of Professional Estate Planning Services:

1. Expert Guidance: Professionals are expert in the intricacies of estate and tax law, offering tailored advice based on your specific needs and goals.

2. Complexity Handled: They can effectively handle complex scenarios that might involve businesses, overseas assets, special needs beneficiaries, or significant tax planning considerations.

3. Peace of Mind: Hiring a professional can give you confidence that your estate plan is precise, sound from a legal point, and efficiently designed to fulfill your intentions.

Cons of Professional Estate Planning Services:

1. Cost: Professional services can be expensive, especially for complex estates, which might be a deterrent for some people.

2. Time: The process can be time-consuming, requiring meetings, discussions, and reviews which might extend over weeks or months.

3. Less Control: Some might feel they have less control over the estate planning process when it is outsourced to a professional.

Making the Right Choice

1. Complexity of the Estate: The more complex your estate, the more advisable it is to seek professional help.

2. Personal Comfort with Legal Matters: If you are not comfortable handling legal documents or do not understand the legal implications fully, professional guidance is recommended.

3. Budget: Consider your budget for estate planning and weigh it against the potential risks of a DIY approach.

Steps to Decide

1. Assess Your Estate: Take stock of your assets, liabilities, and special considerations like business ownership or charitable intentions.

2. Educate Yourself: Understand the basics of estate planning to make an informed decision about what level of professional help you might need.

3. Consult with Professionals: Even if you choose the DIY route, it might be beneficial to have a consultation with a professional to point out any potential issues or additional considerations.

Section 30: Effective Communication and Conflict Management in Estate Planning

Without clear communication and proactive conflict management, even the most well-crafted estate plan can lead to misunderstandings, disputes, and family discord. This section will support you going through the intricacies of managing communication and potential conflicts in the context of estate planning.

The Importance of Open Communication in Estate Planning

Open communication is the cornerstone of successful estate planning. By discussing your plans and intentions with your loved ones, you can prevent misunderstandings and provide clarity about your wishes. Start by having honest and transparent conversations with your immediate family members. Explain the reasoning behind your decisions and how you intend to distribute your assets. This transparency helps set expectations and reduces the likelihood of surprises that can lead to conflict.

In these discussions, emphasize your goals and values. Explain why certain decisions were made and how they align with your overall vision for your family's future. Encourage your family members to ask questions and express their concerns. Addressing these issues early on can help prevent them from escalating into larger disputes later.

Involving Key Family Members and Advisors

Involving key family members and advisors in the estate planning process is essential for fostering understanding and cooperation. Invite your children, spouse, and other significant family members to participate in discussions about your estate plan. This involvement guarantees that all parties are aligned and informed about your intentions.

Experts like estate planning lawyers, financial advisors, and accountants can offer helpful advice and insights. These experts can help clarify complex legal and financial issues, making it easier for your family to understand your plan. Their involvement also adds a layer of impartiality, which can be crucial in managing potential conflicts.

When working with advisors, ensure that they have a comprehensive understanding of your family dynamics and goals. This understanding enables them to provide tailored advice and assist you in crafting a strategy that reduces the potential for disputes.

Addressing Potential Sources of Conflict

Identifying and addressing potential sources of conflict is a proactive approach to managing estate planning. Common sources of conflict include perceived inequalities in asset distribution, misunderstandings about the roles and responsibilities of executors and trustees, and differing opinions about the care of dependents.

To address these issues, clearly outline your reasoning in your estate plan. For instance, if you intend to allocate a larger slice of your estate to one kid due to their financial need or caregiving role, explain this decision in a letter of intent or family meeting. Transparency helps your beneficiaries understand your intentions and reduces the potential for feelings of resentment or unfairness.

Consider including conflict resolution mechanisms in your estate plan. These mechanisms, such as mediation or arbitration clauses, provide a structured way to resolve disputes without resorting to litigation. By outlining a clear process for handling disagreements, you can help prevent conflicts from escalating and preserve family harmony.

Preparing for Difficult Conversations

Preparing for difficult conversations about your estate plan requires sensitivity and tact. Approach these discussions with empathy and understanding, recognizing that your family members may have strong emotions and opinions. Choose a time and place that allows for open and uninterrupted dialogue.

Begin by explaining the significance of estate planning and your commitment to ensuring that your wishes are respected. Share your plan and invite feedback, making it clear that you value their input and want to address any concerns they may have. Listening actively and validating their feelings can help build trust and cooperation.

If you anticipate significant disagreements, consider using a professional mediator to facilitate the conversation. A neutral third party can help keep the discussion focused and constructive, ensuring that everyone's perspectives are heard and considered.

Documenting Your Decisions and Intentions

Documenting your decisions and intentions clearly in your estate plan is essential for preventing misunderstandings and disputes. Ensure that your will, trusts, and other legal documents are detailed and unambiguous. Include specific instructions for asset distribution, the roles and responsibilities of executors and trustees, and any other important aspects of your plan.

Consider writing a letter of intent to accompany your legal documents. This letter can provide additional context and explain the reasoning behind your decisions. While not legally binding, it serves as a valuable guide for your family and advisors, helping them understand your intentions and carry out your wishes faithfully.

Consistently reassess and revise your estate plan to align with changes in your life. Keeping your plan current ensures that it remains relevant and effective, reducing the potential for confusion and conflict.

Section 31: Document Execution in Estate Planning: Signature, Notarization, Witnesses, and Storage

Estate planning involves more than just drafting wills and trusts. The execution of these documents is critical to ensure they are legally binding and effective. This process includes understanding local requirements, registering documents, having witnesses, and making copies. Let's delve into these aspects to provide a comprehensive understanding of how to properly execute your estate planning documents.

Execution

Local Requirements

Every state or jurisdiction has specific requirements for the execution of estate planning documents. These requirements ensure that the documents are legally valid and enforceable. Generally, you must sign your will and other estate planning documents in the presence of witnesses, and sometimes a notary public, depending on the document type and local regulations. In many places, a will must be signed in the presence of at least two witnesses who are not beneficiaries of the will. These witnesses must observe you signing the will and must sign the document themselves to attest that they witnessed your signature. This process helps prevent fraud and undue influence, ensuring that the document truly reflects your wishes.

Creating trusts, powers of attorney, and other estate planning documents may each have their own specific requirements. Some states require notarization for these documents, while others do not. It's key to consult with an estate planning expert to uncover the specific requirements in your jurisdiction. Adhering to these requirements is essential to avoid any challenges to the validity of your documents.

Documents Registration

Registering your estate planning documents, like a will or trust, might not be mandatory, but it can be a prudent step to ensure they are recognized and easily accessible. For instance, some states offer the option to file your will with the local probate court while you are still alive. This ensures that the document is stored safely and can be easily located after your death.

For trusts and powers of attorney, registration is less common but can still be beneficial in some cases, particularly if the documents involve real estate or other significant assets. Registering these documents can provide an additional layer of authenticity and security, helping to ensure that they are honored by financial institutions and other entities.

Witnesses

Witnesses are important in the process of completing the estate planning documents. Their presence and signature help ensure that the documents are valid and that the wishes of the person creating the estate plan are accurately represented. Witnesses provide an extra layer of verification that you, the testator, were of sound mind and not under duress when signing the document. Choosing the right witnesses is important; they should be individuals who are impartial and not beneficiaries of the will to avoid any potential conflicts of interest.

When selecting witnesses, consider their availability and willingness to testify if your will is ever contested. Ideally, witnesses should be younger than you and likely to outlive you, ensuring they can serve their purpose if needed. Their signatures, alongside yours, make the document more robust against legal challenges.

Making Copies

After executing your estate planning documents, making copies is an essential step. While the original documents hold the most legal weight, having copies can be invaluable for reference and ensuring your wishes are known and accessible. Provide copies to your executor, trustees, and any other individuals who have a role in your estate plan. This makes sure that everyone knows what they need to do and can respond quickly when needed.

Storing these copies securely is also important. Keep them in a safe place where they can be easily retrieved when needed. This might include safes, deposit boxes, or with your attorney. Make sure to inform your executor and key family members where these documents are stored to prevent any confusion or delays in accessing them.

Safeguarding Your Estate Planning Documents: Strategies for Secure Storage

Storing your estate planning documents correctly is just as crucial as creating them initially. Ensuring that your documents are safe, well-organized, and accessible to those who need them is crucial for effective estate management. Here we will cover various aspects of document storage, including labeling and organization, the use of safes, deposit boxes, and attorneys, as well as other innovative methods to keep your documents secure.

Labeling and Organization

Effective labeling and organization are foundational to managing your estate planning documents. Start by compiling a thorough list of all your important documents, including your will, trusts, powers of attorney, health care directives, and financial statements. Each document should be clearly labeled and organized in a way that is intuitive for those who will need to access them.

Consider using a filing system that categorizes documents by type or function. For instance, have separate folders for legal documents, financial records, medical directives, and personal letters. Use labels that are clear and specific, such as "Last Will and Testament," "Living Trust," "Health Care Proxy," and "Financial Power of Attorney." This organization helps ensure that your executor and loved ones can quickly locate the necessary documents without confusion or delay.

Also, maintaining a central document where you note all your important documents and where they are stored. This list should include the names and contact information of your advisors, such as your attorney, financial planner, and accountant. Providing a roadmap of where everything is stored can save time and reduce stress during critical moments.

Safes

One of the most secure places to store your estate planning documents is a home safe. A safe provides protection against theft, fire, and natural disasters. When choosing a safe, consider one that is fireproof and waterproof, ensuring that your documents remain intact under extreme conditions.

Place the safe in a discreet but accessible location within your home. Inform your executor, spouse, or a trusted family member about the safe's existence and how to access it. Ensure they are aware of the combination or possess the key. For added security, you can also use a safe deposit box in conjunction with your home safe, splitting your documents between the two locations.

Deposit Boxes

Safe deposit boxes at a bank offer a high level of security for storing your important documents. These boxes are typically located in a vault, providing robust protection against theft and damage. Using a safe deposit box ensures that your documents are stored in a controlled environment with multiple layers of security.

However, there are some considerations to keep in mind. Access to a safe deposit box can be restricted if you pass away or become incapacitated, as banks may require legal proof before allowing access. To mitigate this, ensure that your executor or a trusted individual is named on the box and has the legal authority to access it. This can be arranged through the bank by adding a joint renter or authorized signer.

Attorneys

Storing your estate planning documents with your attorney is another secure option. Attorneys often provide secure storage for original documents as part of their services. This ensures that your documents are kept in a professional and secure environment, and they can be easily accessed when needed.

Make sure to inform your executor and important family members about where your attorney has stored your documents. Provide them with the contact information for your attorney's office and ensure they know that the documents can be retrieved from there. This method also allows for seamless updates to your documents, as your attorney can quickly access and amend them as necessary.

Other Ways

In addition to the traditional methods, you can use other innovative methods to store and protect your estate planning documents:

1. Digital Storage: Scanning your documents and storing them digitally can provide a convenient backup. Use secure cloud storage services that offer encryption and multi-factor authentication to protect your digital files. Ensure that your executor and trusted family members have access to these digital records by sharing the necessary login information.

2. Secure Document Storage Services: Some companies specialize in secure document storage, offering both physical and digital solutions. These services often provide features like fireproof and waterproof storage, 24/7 security, and online access to scanned copies of your documents.

3. Hybrid Approach: Combining multiple storage methods can enhance security and accessibility. For instance, you might keep originals in a safe deposit box, copies in a home safe, and digital versions stored securely online. This redundancy ensures that your documents are protected against various risks and are accessible when needed.

Section 32: Navigating the Estate Administration Process

Upon a person's death, their estate must be managed in accordance with their will or, if there is no will, according to state intestacy laws. Estate administration involves a series of steps to guarantee the deceased's intentions are fulfilled and that legal and financial obligations are met. This process is typically overseen by an executor named in the will, or an administrator appointed by the court if there is no will.

Initiating the Estate Administration Process

The estate administration process begins with filing the will with the probate court. Without a will, the court assigns an administrator to oversee the estate. The first step for the executor or administrator is to gather and organize all relevant documents, including the death certificate, financial statements, will, property deeds, as well as all other pertinent records.

Once the will is filed and the executor is officially appointed, the court issues letters of testamentary or letters of administration, providing the executor legal permission to manage the estate. This legal authority is essential for accessing the departed's assets, closing debts, and managing the estate's affairs.

Understanding the Difference Between an Administrator and an Executor

In the context of estate planning and probate, the roles of an executor and an administrator are crucial but distinct. Both oversee the management of a deceased person's estate, yet their appointments and responsibilities differ based on the presence of a will and the specific circumstances surrounding the estate.

Executor

An executor is an individual named in a will to administer the estate of the deceased. The executor's primary duty involves guaranteeing that the departed's wishes, as specified in their will, are faithfully carried out. Here are the key aspects of the role:

1. Appointment: An executor is explicitly designated by the dead person in their will. The will typically includes a clause naming the executor and, often, a backup executor if the primary one cannot or will not serve.

2. Duties: As an executor, your responsibilities involve finding and assessing the assets left by the deceased, settling any outstanding debts and taxes, and then distributing what's left to the beneficiaries according to the instructions laid out in the will. The executor also handles the probate process, which involves validating the will in court.

3. Authority: Executors have the power to manage the estate as soon as they are officially appointed by the probate court. This involves managing the estate's financial affairs, including closing bank accounts, selling property if necessary, and handling any legal claims against the estate.

4. Challenges: Executors can face challenges, particularly if the will is contested or if beneficiaries have disagreements. It is the executor's responsibility to manage these issues while adhering to the deceased's wishes.

Administrator

Conversely, an administrator is appointed by the court when no will exists, the will lacks an executor, or the appointed executor is incapable or does not want to serve. The function of an administrator is similar to that of an executor but comes with some notable differences:

1. Appointment: An administrator is appointed by the probate court, typically following a hierarchy of eligible individuals. This hierarchy usually starts with the surviving spouse, followed by adult children, other close relatives, and, if necessary, creditors.

2. Duties: The duties of an administrator mirror those of an executor and include inventorying and valuing the estate's assets, closing off debts and taxes, and allocating the residual assets to the rightful heirs. Since there is no will, the distribution follows state intestacy laws, which dictate how assets should be divided among surviving family members.

3. Authority: Administrators gain their authority from the court after filing a petition and being officially appointed. They receive letters of administration, which grant them the legal power to manage the estate's affairs.

4. Challenges: Administrators often face challenges due to the absence of a will, which can lead to disputes among heirs and complications in determining how the assets should be distributed. They must adhere strictly to state laws and the court's instructions to ensure fair and lawful administration.

Key Differences

The primary differences between an executor and an administrator lie in how they are appointed and the basis of their authority. An executor is chosen by the deceased through a will and follows the directives outlined in that will. In contrast, an administrator is designated by the court and must adhere to state laws of intestacy to distribute the estate. Both roles require a diligent and organized individual capable of handling financial and legal responsibilities, but the presence or absence of a will significantly influences their scope of authority and the framework within which they operate.

Inventory and Appraisal of Assets

A critical part of estate administration is taking an inventory of the deceased's assets. This involves identifying and valuing all estate assets, such as bank accounts, financial holdings, real estate, and personal belongings, and any business interests. The executor must document these assets and their values, often requiring professional appraisals for real estate and valuable personal property.

This inventory provides a clear picture of the estate's valuation, essential for calculating any estate taxes that might be owed. It also helps verify that all assets are identified and properly managed throughout the administration process.

Paying Debts and Taxes

Prior to transferring assets to heirs, the estate needs to first clear any remaining debts and taxes. This includes paying off any loans, credit card bills, and other liabilities, as well as filing and paying income and estate taxes. The executor must inform the deceased's creditors and settling valid claims against the estate.

The estate's funds are used to pay these debts and taxes. If the estate lacks adequate liquid assets to cover these obligations, the executor may need to sell a property or other assets to generate the necessary funds. It is crucial to handle these financial matters promptly to avoid penalties and interest charges.

Distributing the Remaining Assets

After settling all financial obligations like debts and taxes, the executor can then distribute whatever is left to the beneficiaries as specified in the will. This distribution must be carried out with precision, ensuring that each beneficiary receives their designated share. If there is no will, the distribution is made according to state intestacy laws, which typically prioritize spouses, children, and other close relatives.

The executor must also handle any particular bequests (for example gifts of specific personal items) and ensure that these are delivered to the correct beneficiaries. Clear communication with beneficiaries is essential during this process to manage expectations and address any questions or concerns.

Closing the Estate

After all assets are allocated, the final step in the estate administration process is to close the estate. The executor must prepare a final accounting, detailing all transactions that took place during the administration. This accounting is submitted to the probate court for approval, along with a petition to close the estate.

After the court grants final approval, the executor is formally discharged from their duties. This marks the end of the estate administration process, and the estate is officially closed.

Handling Family Disputes

Family disputes can arise during estate administration, particularly when disputes arise over asset distribution or the interpretation of the will. The executor is pivotal in resolving these conflicts and making sure that the process remains fair and transparent. Open communication and mediation can often resolve conflicts without resorting to legal battles, which can drain time and resources.

Dealing with Unique Assets

Unique assets, such as family heirlooms, business interests, or intellectual property, can complicate estate administration. These items often have sentimental value that exceeds their financial worth, making it challenging to divide them equitably among beneficiaries. The executor must carefully consider the deceased's wishes and the beneficiaries' preferences, possibly arranging for appraisals or facilitating buyouts among family members to ensure a fair distribution.

The Role of Professional Advisors

Expert advisors, like estate lawyers, financial planners, and accountants have a vital part in the estate administration. They provide the expertise needed to navigate complex legal and financial issues, ensuring that the estate is administered effectively and in accordance with all relevant laws. Engaging these professionals early in the process can help prevent mistakes and streamline the administration.

Conclusion

Estate planning is a dynamic and intricate process that encompasses much more than just the distribution of assets. It involves strategic planning, legal considerations, and continuous adaptation to make sure that your vision is honored and the ones you care about are supported. Throughout this book, we have discussed several aspects of estate planning, from the basics of wills and trusts to the complexities of cross-border estates and digital assets. The goal has been to equip you with the knowledge and tools needed to create a comprehensive and effective estate plan.

At its core, estate planning is about preparing for the future. It involves making deliberate decisions today to secure your legacy and provide for the ones you care for tomorrow. A comprehensive estate plan addresses multiple facets of your life and assets, ensuring that nothing is overlooked. This includes managing real estate, financial investments, business interests, digital assets, and even unconventional holdings like art and collectibles.

One of the key themes throughout this book is the importance of flexibility and adaptability in estate planning. Life is unpredictable, and your circumstances, goals, and assets can change over time. An good estate plan is not static; it changes with you. Frequently revising and amending your estate plan is crucial to make sure that it stays aligned with your present situation and wishes.

This flexibility extends to the legal and financial structures you use in your estate plan. Whether through the use of revocable trusts, strategic gifting, or life insurance policies, incorporating mechanisms that allow for adjustments can help manage risks and capitalize on opportunities as they arise.

While this book provides a comprehensive overview of estate planning, the intricacies of your individual situation may require specialized advice. Engaging with experienced legal and financial advisors is essential to go through the intricacies of estate planning successfully. These specialists can offer tailored advice, make sure you are compliant with relevant laws, and help you implement strategies that maximize growth and protection. This is especially important for international assets.

Effective estate planning also involves clear communication and transparency with your loved ones. Talking about your strategies and intentions with your family can avoid misunderstandings and potential disputes. It helps ensure that everyone is on the same page and understands the reasoning behind your decisions. This openness can foster trust and cooperation, making the administration of your estate smoother and more efficient.

Ultimately, the purpose of estate planning is to secure your legacy. It is about more than just the distribution of wealth; it is about ensuring that your values, wishes, and intentions are carried forward. Whether through charitable giving, providing for future generations, or preserving family heirlooms, your estate plan is a reflection of what is important to you.

By taking the time to plan thoughtfully and comprehensively, you can establish a legacy that endures, providing security and support for your beloved and making a lasting impact.

Estate planning is something that needs careful thinking, wise decision-making, and regular attention. It is a critical component of financial planning and personal responsibility. As you move forward, remember that the foundation of a successful estate plan is built on understanding your goals, leveraging the right tools and strategies, and seeking professional guidance when needed.

This book has provided you with a roadmap to navigate the intricacies of estate planning. Armed with this knowledge, you are now better equipped to create an estate plan that reflects your values, protects your assets, and secures your legacy for the future.

Thank You!

Thank you for choosing "Estate Planning and Living Trusts Blueprint" and for embarking on this journey with us. Your engagement and feedback are invaluable, not just to us, but to the entire community of readers who are on this path of discovery and empowerment. Each piece of feedback enriches our collective experience and understanding. We are deeply grateful for your contributions and enthusiasm. It's supporters like you who make this endeavor so rewarding and meaningful. Here is what you can do to share your feedback:

Option A - Create a short video: Show off your new book and share your impressions.

Option B - Post a photo (or photos): Capture your copy of the book in a creative way and add a few words to share your thoughts.

Option C - Just Write: If you prefer to express yourself just in writing, a few thoughtful sentences reflecting on what you have read would be greatly appreciated.

Thank you once again for being such an integral part of our community and for helping us spread knowledge that can change lives. Please note that this is entirely optional.

Scan the QR code below to leave your review:

Access Your Bonus Content

As a token of our appreciation, we are offering you exclusive bonus content to further assist you in designing your Estate Plan:

Scan the QR code or go to the link below to get your bonus content

Or go to the following link → rebrand.ly/et-extra

References

- Bruce R. Hopkins. "Starting and Managing a Nonprofit Organization", Wiley, 2009
- business-money.com
- "CFP Board Financial Planning Competency Handbook", Wiley, 2015
- clemonslaw.com
- digitalcommons.law.uidaho.edu
- ejcl.org
- fastercapital.com
- "Financial Valuation", Wiley, 2012
- forbes.com
- getsnug.com
- Harvey W. Rubin. "Dictionary of Insurance Terms / Fachbegriffe Versicherungswesen", Springer Science and Business Media LLC, 1994
- insight2wealth.com
- investopedia.com
- irs.gov
- Jeffrey H. Rattiner. "Rattiner's Secrets of Financial Planning", Wiley, 2020
- Joan T Erber. "Aging and Older Adulthood", Wiley, 2019
- John J. Vento. "Financial Independence (Getting to Point X)", Wiley, 2018
- kaplaw.com
- Keith R. Fevurly. "Plan Your Financial Future",Springer Science and Business Media LLC, 2013
- legalees.com
- losangelesprobaterealestatesales.com
- Mary Louis Fallows, Rita J. Simon, William Rau. "Public Attitudes About Property Distribution at Death and Intestate Succession Laws in the United States", American Bar Foundation Research Journal, 2018
- middlebury.org
- mlrpc.com
- "Personal Financial Planning for Executives and Entrepreneurs", Springer Science and Business Media LLC, 2018
- ROBERT M. KOZUB. "Special Valuation of Farmland and Closely Held Business Realty for Estate Tax Purposes", Growth and Change, 7/1984
- Ross Levin. "Estate Planning (Distribution)", Wiley, 2012 William Bischoff. "Cut Your Client's Tax Bill", Wiley, 2020
- sandiegoestateplanninglawyerblog.com
- Susan M. Tillery, Thomas N. Tillery. "Essentials of Personal Financial Planning", Wiley, 2017
- "Swiss Annuities and Life Insurance", Wiley, 2012
- Ulrich Schreiber. "International Company Taxation", Springer Nature, 2013
- Walter N. Thorp. "Special Needs—Special Plans", Journal of Disability Policy Studies,2016

Made in the USA
Columbia, SC
25 September 2024

43035269R00076